A
SHATTERED
GLASS

TATE PUBLISHING, LLC

Published in the United States of America
By TATE PUBLISHING, LLC
All Rights Reserved
Do Not Duplicate Without Permission.

All Scripture References are King James Version,
unless otherwise indicated.

Book Design by: TATE PUBLISHING, LLC.

Printed in the United States of America by
TATE PUBLISHING, LLC.
1716 West State Highway 152
Mustang, OK 73064

Publisher's Cataloging in Publication

Wingo, Kathy
   A Shattered Glass/ Kathy Wingo
   Originally Published: Henderson, TN: Hester Publications: 2002
   1. Spiritual Life 2. Family 3. Self-Help
   ISBN-0-9740939-7-1 $14.95

Copyright 2003
Kathy Wingo
Printed in October 2003

A SHATTERED GLASS

"A Life Put Back Together By The Power Of God"

Author: Kathy Wingo

DEDICATION

To

the abused,

broken hearted, abandoned, trapped and hopeless

women of the world.

And to. . . .

God the Father, my Lord and Savior Jesus Christ, who sees each tear drop, knows every heartache and feels each pain. Heaven did indeed hear each whisper. I thank you Jesus, for hearing my cry and bringing me out of the pits of hell.

My loving husband, Richard, who is constantly in prayer with me. You always believe that God hears our prayers. You smile and cry with me when the times are good and also when the times are bad. Thank you for having faith in me. I will walk with you wherever God leads us. Do not ever doubt that you are the strong fresh breath of wind that I feel under me whenever I spread my wings. Thank you for your love and support as we face the battles of life.

My brothers and sisters, whom I love very deeply. We went through so much heartache together growing up, but thank God we made it. I will always appreciate your love and support.

Mama Grace, a great prayer warrior, who embraced me with showers of love when I was so desperate for someone to love me.

My former teachers: Mr. Jerry Johnson, my fifth grade teacher, who saw something in me and encouraged me to work for my dreams. Mrs. Kay Kemp, my sixth grade teacher, who always encouraged me to know that I could make it in life. She taught me to hold my head up and that I could be anything I wanted, if I kept a positive attitude.

ACKNOWLEDGMENTS

Thank you Mary, Rita, Brenda, Sally and Cheryl for always being best friends to me through the years. Your love and support has kept me going.

Words are not enough to express my gratitude to Dr. Lowell Robison and staff from Memphis, Tennessee. Thank you for your loving care for the past fourteen years.

I want to thank Pa and Ma McAdoo for loving me. Your kindness and caring has deeply touched my soul.

To my Texas friends, Syd and Kathy, for accepting me as family.

Mr. Sidney Bolick, author and friend, thank you for sharing your literary expertise.

There are a number of wonderful friends who contributed in countless ways and offered prayers in expression of their love for me as I was writing this book. To you I say, "Thank you from the depths of my heart."

Contents

CHAPTER		PAGE
	Foreword	
1.	Poor House	13
2.	Eating Out Of The Dump	23
3.	Special Child	27
4.	Cathouse	35
5.	That Stuff Wasn't for Kids	41
6,	Sharecropper	47
7.	Hole in the Wall	51
8.	Sold for a Sack of Potatoes	53
9.	From the Frying Pan into the Fire	59
10.	Be Quiet, Dogs	67
11.	Good Old Maverick	71
12.	Where's Harry?	81
13.	Good Bye Daddy	85
14.	On the Run	89
15.	Finally, Enough Courage	101
16.	Rough Days	107
17.	Healing	115
18.	A Mother's Love	127
19.	Mama Grace	137
20.	Three Confirmations	145
21.	Midnight-Knock on the Door	165
22.	Shattered Glass	173
	Epilogue	

FOREWORD

Today, Kathy, a tall, attractive, green eyed, auburn haired lady in her mid-forty's is everything a husband could desire a wife to be. She is a caring mother, grandmother and step-mom. She is my prayer partner, my soul mate, my best friend and most affectionate wife. Gifted with a compassionate heart, Kathy never hesitates to give someone down and out a helping hand, her last $20 or the coat off her back.

She has a Christian charm that can only come from God. Kat, as we all call her, is the center of attraction when we are among friends as they never tire of hearing her tell of her experiences, not only tragic, but most often outrageously humorous.

A true blessing from heaven, Kat is obviously one of God's special children as evidenced by her miraculous ability to accept her past.

My prayer is that by reading her story many who have suffered similar experiences will recognize that total healing and deliverance can only occur through an unfailing faith in God above and His Son Jesus Christ.

Kathy's husband,
Richard Wingo

1
Poor House

I came from a family of nineteen brothers and sisters. Mother always said there were nineteen of us; I can only remember fifteen though. Four of the oldest kids died at an early age or at childbirth, I guess, and four of the oldest children were gone and married while I was still a young child. So I can only remember eleven of us at home doing things together, seven boys and four of us girls. Out of nineteen children, I was the tenth child born. Of the eleven children still at home I was fifth from the oldest.

We were raised in the small community, "out in the sticks," of Whiterose, Tennessee with a population of about three hundred people. There was nothing but dirt roads, woods, gullies and farmland. Whenever someone was coming around the curve down the long dusty dirt road, we knew they were coming to our house, because there were no other houses on the road. We were very poor, our parents liked to drink and their drunkenness was a part of our lives.

My mama's husband's name was Leroy Telson; we children called him Rozen. He was supposed to have been my daddy. Everybody in the county said that Rozen was the best horse trader around especially if he had been drinking. You had to be really careful trading with Rozen or he would cheat you and I mean, really careful. The talk around the community about Rozen was that he had his bunch of kids trained so well to fear the razor strap, that he could work them like slaves, and he did. We all were a good bunch of kids, but had it hard on Telson Hill. Rozen would buy land cheap that was nothing but trees, stumps and gullies and put us kids to work clearing it off, trying to make decent farmland out of it. Rozen was a rounder; whenever he wasn't horse trading or farming, he was bootlegging and gambling. He had a wild streak in him and Rozen loved women, any women.

Us children were very close as brothers and sisters; we did everything together. We chopped cotton together in the fields when it was in season and hauled hay. About four in the morning, we got up to do a day's work before going to school. The boys would go to the barn, feed and milk the cows, slop the hogs, feed the chickens, and water the livestock. The girls cooked breakfast, one fixing biscuits, one cooking the meat, one cooking eggs with gravy and one setting the table. After breakfast, we did the dishes and washed the clothes on an old hand wringer washing machine, then hung the clothes on an old rusty barbwire fence. The girls washed the clothes in the morning so they would have time to dry outside during the daytime hours; then made the beds and swept the floors before getting ready for school. Our small, poor house was about a mile from the main highway and we had to walk that long gravel road every day to catch the school bus. On rare occasions if we were running late, Rozen would load us up in the truck and take us to catch the bus. Rozen usually had the truck left at the end of the road in the afternoon for us to ride home. One of the boys would drive the old truck down the long dusty road to the house. Rozen knew if we had a ride we could get started to work earlier in the afternoons before it got nighttime.

We had eighty-six acres of land on the farm and Rozen would always take us to the fields early in the morning, sharpen our hoes for us to chop cotton and sit at the end of the row under the shade tree with an iced keg of beer. While we worked, he drank. If we would miss or skip a row, or chop too much cotton down, he would get a limb, strip the branches off of the limb to make a switch to beat us with. It would be so hot and we would hurry to get our row out so we could have a cold drink of water. We were taught as children to work hard, Rozen always said, "You haven't done any work, until you have sweated." It made us tough; it made us the people that we are today.

We didn't have much love at home, but we kids had love inside of us and we were humble. We always wanted to share that love; hoping that if we did, we would get it back. I love my brothers and sisters very much; we went through hard times together growing up and this made us close. It didn't matter that we did not have many friends when we were children because we had each other and we stuck together. It was hard to have friends when we lived in the sticks and worked all the time, besides, who would want to visit Telson's poor house.

I loved my mama very much, but there were times that I didn't like her. I couldn't understand why Mama kept having a baby almost every twelve months. After all, she wasn't the one that took care of them. We kids took care of each other. We were the ones that changed and washed all the nasty diapers, not Mama. If she changed one she would throw it in a bucket in the backyard for us to rinse out before we put it in the old washing machine. It was a strain on us, Mama having a child almost every twelve months. Mama always said, "Having a baby is no more that having a bowel movement." I guess that was right because she had her first child at the age of thirteen and they just kept on coming.

There were cracks in the floors of our house where you could see the chickens playing underneath, and it was very cold in the wintertime. We all would gather around the old potbelly wood stove; that was the only place in the house where it was halfway warm. It was so cold even the mice would come and gather around the fire. I remember one night my brother and his girlfriend, Tracy, were sitting in the living room when they were dating. They had the light off and had been very quiet. They heard a scratching noise, turned the light on and when they did there were several mice sitting in front of the old wood stove trying to keep warm. Can you imagine, courting someone while watching mice play around the fire?

It was the boy's responsibility to keep plenty of wood racked up on the front porch for the old stove. They usually had wood piled all the way to the ceiling. During cold weather they would cut down trees in the back pastures almost every Saturday morning for firewood. All they had was an old crosscut hand saw and a couple of chopping axes, but they kept us in plenty of firewood. Once they did have an old chain saw that smoked a lot, but it stayed tore up most of the time.

Our neighbors, the Robinson family, gathered up some clothes and blankets for our family. We had lots of blankets piled up in layers on our beds to stay warm. There would be four of us girls in the same bed, and three or four boys in their bed, the other boys slept on a mattress in the floor. We usually would get to playing and fighting over the covers and pillows until Rozen would holler out at us, "Y'all better be quiet in there or I'll be in there with the belt." Sometimes we would get to laughing underneath the covers, hoping Rozen wouldn't hear us. The boys would be "sittin on frogs," our saying for passing gas, until we would just die with laughter. Brothers and sisters slept in the same bedroom when we were younger. We did have some good times together.

Our bathroom was an old one-seater outhouse in the backyard. It always gave me an eerie feeling because I was always afraid that I was going to fall down in that hole. The hole was bigger than I was. There was no paper, just an old Sears and Roebuck catalog. There was no running water in the house; we had an outside well to draw water from. We had a long well bucket tied to a rope that hung over a well pulley. The rope then attached to a crank. We had to let the bucket drop down into the well until we heard it splash in the water, give it time to fill up, then crank the bucket back up. We then held the well bucket over the water bucket and pulled the ring on the top of the well bucket to let the water run out. We carried buckets, several at a time, to put on the old wood burning stove to heat up water for a hot bath. We had a galvanized

The "Poor House" Back Home

washtub that looked like a cow-watering trough that we took a bath in. The girls would use the water first and then the boys. We didn't have regular good smelling soap; we used some stuff that we had cooked up called lye soap. It was made from hog fat and lye. We would cook it in an old black iron kettle and then as it cooled it thickened. We would then cut it into soap bars. It didn't make any bubbles but it "sure got you clean." We had to be careful and not get it in our eyes, because it would burn like fire.

I can remember my brothers going hunting. This was a special event because it usually meant we had meat to eat for a while. They would kill squirrels, rabbits, deer, coon, possum, anything that walked, ran, or crawled. We usually had biscuits and gravy with whatever they brought home. That sure was some good eating. In the fall, we would kill hogs and a goat or two to eat through the winter. For Thanksgiving and Christmas we would have turkey and fried chicken along with white beans and potatoes. About the only thing we always had plenty of was flour, cornmeal, big sticks of butter, cheese, powdered milk, and powdered eggs. These came from the welfare commodities we got once a month.

We would kill and eat chicken about once a month. We kids had to chop the heads off the chickens with an ax. It was an awful feeling seeing those poor chickens flop around with no heads. We would have a big kettle over the fire boiling the water to scald the chicken feathers off. I hated to pluck those nasty, stinking feathers out one at a time. However, by the time we fried and ate them we forgot about the suffering that those poor chickens went through. We would kill several chickens at one killing to feed us all, but that didn't guarantee us kids getting a chicken leg. We had to wait until the grown-ups ate first. Sometimes there might have been an old chicken neck, back or wing left for us to eat. I hated getting "them old bone pieces," but we always got the leftovers. Rozen let his drinking buddies eat first, usually that was the reason we had the chicken dinner in the first place.

After all of the drunks and Rozen got through eating, they went into the backyard to the old smokehouse to gamble. Many times I wanted to tell the law about what was going on, but part of them was the law. Everybody in the county knew about Telson Hill. It was a place of bootlegged whiskey, beer drinking, gambling, fighting and a bunch of raggedy kids hanging around. The drunks and gamblers did like all the pretty girls that lived on the hill.

Some folks said the Telson girls were the prettiest girls in the county. We may have been poor and raggedy looking, but when I was about ten I won second maid in the school beauty review. Our neighbor down the road, Mrs. Thelma Welch had a daughter the same age as me, and she had let me wear some of her daughter's clothes. Mrs. Thelma had rolled my hair and fixed it in long lock curls hanging down my back. She tied a pink ribbon in my hair that hung down to the end of my long curls. I wore a pink satin dress with a big bow tied in the back over a big can-can slip with a hoop in it to make it stand out; white patent leather shoes and white lacy socks. I was so happy that I had won second place; I felt as pretty as the other girls in my class at school. Because we were the winners in the beauty review, three other girls and I got to ride on the back of a convertible in the parade at the county fair. We rode down the street waving at the people and throwing candy to them. It was a special time for me, and I will always remember it. This was probably the first time I had on good underwear that wasn't full of holes. I really hated returning the clothes back to Mrs. Thelma after I wore them the second time in the parade. It was fun while it lasted. I always wished for just one nice outfit of my own, something that nobody had ever worn. I was so grateful Mrs. Thelma took the time to fix me up for the beauty review and the parade; she was a very compassionate person and was always trying to help us poor kids on Telson Hill.

My younger sister Sharon also won queen a couple of years later. Our oldest sister Camille, who was already married and gone from home, had fixed Sharon up for the elementary beauty review. Camille had rolled Sharon's hair on rollers made from stretching out the wound up tin left over after opening a potted meat can. We would take the spiraled tin, cut it up in several six inch pieces, wrap cloth around each piece several times, roll our hair up and bend the ends under so they would stay in our hair until our hair dried. After we took them out of our hair our hair would fall down in thick curls. Sharon wore a pretty cream dress with burgundy trim that had a hoop in it and white patent leather shoes. I remember so well what we wore because these were the best clothes we ever had worn, even though they were borrowed. Another older sister, Diane was in the top ten finalists in a beauty revue when she was in high school. She wore a pretty blue chiffon lace floor length gown with long white gloves reaching past her elbows. She was very pretty and I thought she should have won because, to me, she was as pretty as any of the other girls, but I realized early in life that everybody can't be a winner, especially if you came from Telson Hill.

Mama and Rozen would lose what little bit of money they had on Saturday and Sunday nights gambling in the back yard in the smokehouse. Monday morning would come; "they would be broke" and have nothing but a hangover, and no money for us kids to eat school lunches. So we got jobs in the school cafeteria to pay for our lunches. That was one sure way of us getting to eat. The girls would wipe off the tables; the boys would carry out the garbage cans, sweep, and mop the lunchroom floors. The school knew the kind of home we came from and would always help us kids out by giving us whatever jobs were available. The Telsons were just about the total cafeteria clean-up crew. The other kids would be outside having recess while we were working in the lunchroom. We all knew nothing was free in life for us, so we worked at school to eat lunch.

We had to make our own way. We felt degraded, but the whole school knew we were very, very poor. We did the best we knew how. I always said to myself, "Someday we will be grown up and things will be different." There was a lot of days Rozen would keep us out of school to work; it didn't make any difference if we had a test that day or whatever, if he said stay home that day, you stayed home, didn't ask any questions and went to work. Rozen never kept all of us home the same day; he didn't want the welfare department after him and knew some of us had to be at school. We all couldn't be sick at the same time; you know what I mean. He was the rooster that crowed and believe me we all knew it!

Each of us girls always wanted a pretty new doll to play with, one we could call our own. All I ever had was some paper dolls I cut out of a magazine or an old used doll with matted hair and ragged clothes. At Christmas we would have a Christmas tree; the boys would go out into the woods and cut a cedar tree. We would put it in a bucket of dirt to hold it up and fill it up with water so it wouldn't get so dry. We never had lights on it. We would pop corn, thread a needle, and make strings of popcorn to put all the way around the tree. We would pick up pinecones and string them on the tree also. We would take paper, color and fold it to make star ornaments. We thought they were just as pretty as store bought. We longed just to have the simple things in life. I can't remember ever having a bicycle, dog or cat; we were lucky to get ourselves fed, much less some stray animal. At Christmas we would get a little something under the tree, usually used toys and dolls the neighbors didn't want anymore. The local Baptist Church, where we kids went with Mrs. Betty Cole, would sometimes bring us a Christmas basket and some clothes, which were usually heavy coats for the smaller kids.

2
Eating Out Of The Dump

If we were lucky, we would get some fruit and candy, but it wasn't always fresh. Rozen would go to the local grocery stores and ask when they were going to throw the outdated stuff away, he would tell them that he needed it to feed his house full of hungry kids, so they would tell Rozen when they were taking it to the dump. Rozen would always go to the dump the day the outdated groceries were thrown out, load them up in his old truck and bring them home for us kids to sort out the good from the bad. He always said most of it was still eatable; we just had to wash the produce real good and cut the bad spots out. Usually there would be some bent up canned goods, but they would still open. The stuff in the boxes was usually pretty good, unless we found cockroaches in it, but a few bugs never bothered Rozen.

At the age of thirteen I dreamed of wearing a little bit of makeup or at least a little lipstick. The other girls at school were starting to wear makeup along with nylon panty hose, but we didn't have any money for personal things, so I just dreamed of looking pretty. Mama always said, "A little paint will help any old barn look better," so I thought it would make me look more attractive and I wanted to look like mama because I always thought my mama was one of the prettiest women in the whole wide world. When I went to the fields to work, I would sometimes pick polkberries, mash out the red juice and put it on my cheeks and lips. I wanted my cheeks to look a soft rosy red. Sometimes I would steal some of mama's red lipstick out of her purse and put it on my lips. What I really liked was to get her face powder and put it on my face. I liked it all over my face because it felt so smooth. One time she caught me getting into her makeup, she took off her high heel shoe, hit me hard with it, leaving a big goose egg on top of my head. Mama was really mad at me, she said, "You know better than to bother my stuff, you d _ _ _ brat." I always wished she wouldn't talk so ugly to me.

When I started my menstrual cycle we didn't have money for sanitary napkins so we used old rags put together to be thick enough for a pad. We just had to make do with whatever we had. My underclothes were so raggedy that I had about five or six holes in my underwear and usually a yellow dingy bra that was two sizes too small. I always got the hand-me-downs and by the time I got them they were worn out.

When summer time came it was hot as heck. We didn't have any air conditioner, just one big box fan in the middle of the house, and it was usually turned toward Rozen's room and no air circulated toward us "kid's room." We had the windows up and the flies were coming in. There were no screens on the windows because we were too poor to have any. We could fight the insects coming in the house better than not getting any cool air. So we just left the windows open. It seemed like some days it was a hundred and ten degrees, and you could really smell the hog pen and chicken yard. We just about had to put our heads under the cover to keep from smelling the terrible odor, but it was too hot to have cover. We couldn't win for losing. We kids couldn't wait for the weather to get cooler; we could always keep warmer in the wintertime by putting on more clothes, but in the summer time there was not much of a way to stay cool unless you stayed under one of the big shade trees.

At this time we had no television and no telephone, but we did have electricity. We got to go to the Kemps' house once in a great while to watch a program on television. They lived down the road and thought the world of us kids. They would fix crackers with marshmallows in the stove oven for us because they knew we never got good treats at home.

Mrs. Kemp would always just hug us and acted so proud to see us come. A lot of times she would brush and braid our long hair and put it in pigtails. That always made me feel special because I knew she loved me. The Kemps were the closest thing to grandparents we had.

3
Special Child

I never knew my grandparents on my mother's side. Her daddy was dead and her mother was in prison for fighting and attacking another woman with a butcher knife. I guess mama got her meanness after her. So I really don't know much about Mama's folks. Rozen's father was dead and his mother, Mrs. Pearlee had died when I was nine years old. Ironically, all I can remember of her is that she was a praying woman. She didn't like Rozen drinking and gambling in front of us kids, but she had no control over him. He did whatever he wanted to do. We never did visit her very much. I am very sorry that I was not given the opportunity to spend more time with her. The only thing I remember her saying to me was, "You are a special child of the Lord and His hand will always be on you."

Mrs. Betty Cole, a lady down the road came every Sunday morning to carry us kids to church. She was a strong Christian lady and tried to encourage us kids to go to church and Sunday school. Sometimes she would bring boxes of clothes she had gathered up from different neighbors for us kids to wear. We were proud of anything we got. She had a burden for the kids on Telson Hill.

One hot summer day I was getting ready for church. Mama and Rozen were under the shade tree in the front yard. I was wearing a little red skirt to church and a button was missing off the skirt, so I went outside with a safety pin for mama to pin my skirt. Rozen took the safety pin away from mama, pulled me to him and started sticking the pin in my left breast several times. I cried and said, "Please don't, that hurts!" but he kept on sticking me until I was bleeding. Mama said, "Quit, Rozen!" but he was drunk and slapped her right in the face. After that he squeezed my breast really hard and laughed. His rough hands hurt me so badly. I finally got away from him and went into the house. I hated him because he was so mean and evil. We were scared to death the times he was on a drunken rage. I never asked mama to pin another skirt after that little episode. I was about twelve years old at that time. I blamed mama as much as I did Rozen; she could have taken better care of us kids if she didn't drink also. I guess she had to drink to tolerate Rozen. I just know I did not feel any love from those two. We survived it day by day, but this was just the way life was most of the time on Telson Hill.

Diane, the oldest sister at home, had also suffered physical and mental abuse as I did. The other two girls Sharon and Lesley were a lot younger than Diane and me, so they had a way to go before it got too rough on them. The boys also suffered mental and physical abuse; Rozen would think nothing of picking up a stick or a plow line and knocking the crap out of them. He would get crazy whenever he got mad, especially if he had been drinking, it's a miracle he hadn't killed one of us; mama would always stick up for Rozen regardless of how he treated us kids. I never have understood that, even to this very day. I believe mama loved Rozen better than life itself.

I always felt like I was picked on more than the others. I was born with a slightly short left foot; it caused me to limp when I walked. We couldn't afford good shoes with built up insoles to correct my feet. My balance was bad and everyone teased me and called me "crip." Even in high school some smart mouthed kids, both boys and girls, would call me "tippy-toe" because I walked with such a bad limp. I was so upset that I went to the principal's office; broke down and cried. I explained to him that I had a bad foot that lacked two inches touching the floor and caused me to walk on my toes with a bad limp. I told the principal, "I have a name, Kathy Telson, and I don't like being called tippy-toe or crip, would you please do something about it? I am embarrassed and self conscious about my foot as it is, I am walking the best I can." Mr. Powers, the school principal, gathered all the physical education boys in the gym that Friday morning. He told them, "I'd better not hear of one student calling Kathy Telson any kind of a nickname concerning the way she walks, she has a deformed foot caused at birth. This is not showing respect for her by making fun of something she cannot help. This is cruel, degrading and uncalled for. It had better not ever happen again, if so and if I hear about it you will be brought to my office with the paddle on your behind." That next week at school when someone met me in the hall they didn't even speak. I knew the kids at school were talking and laughing among themselves but I didn't care as long as they didn't call me "tippy-toe" or "crip." It was hard enough to deal with anyway without it being called to my attention all the time. So my school days weren't all that great either.

Mama had always had her pick of us kids and sadly to say, I wasn't one of her favorites. I still longed for mama to give me attention and love regardless of how mean she was to me. Her pick of the girls at that time was Diane, she was the oldest girl still living at home and mama would butter her up because mama had to depend on her to take care of us younger kids; mama would give her a few quarters to watch after us while she went to the beer joints. It appeared mama favored the boys over us girls. I never could understand why, but it is still that way today. I always figured she was ashamed about the way she let Rozen treat us girls.

Most of us kids at about fifteen or sixteen would find someone to marry because we wanted to get out of the abusive poor house and away from Rozen's drinking buddies that hung around our house all of the time.

I can remember as a child, walking the long distance, to catch the school bus, praying, "Lord, there has to be more to life than this; fussing, fighting, drinking, cussing, beatings and just working all the time, from sun up to sun down. Anything beats this kind of rough life." There was always work, in the fields and in the house. There were arguments. Mama and Rozen would drink until they got into an argument and that would lead to a fight. I would slide down under the covers and pray, "Dear Jesus, help me to get out of this." I was so unhappy as a child, but I prayed through it. When we were in the fields we would work hard and sweat like a bunch of dogs. At night, my body was so tired from the hard work and long hours that was required of us.

We always looked forward to sundown so that we could quit working, go back to the house and have a hot supper that was usually cornbread, white beans and stewed potatoes. That is the food we were raised on. We had long benches on each side our dinner table and we would line up like a bunch of hogs at a feed trough to eat because we were always so hungry. There usually was enough for us to eat, but it might not have been what we wanted and maybe not enough for second helpings.

Some days I was told not to go to the fields to work. When I didn't go, I knew that there was a reason. I always got nervous on those days. Rozen always said that I would have to stay home to cook and clean. He would say the girls had to swap up with the house chores so that mama would not have so much to do. I was thirteen years old and looked like I was sixteen or seventeen. I hated that I was so well developed for my age. I always knew when I didn't go to the field that was Rozen's opportunity! I hated so much for him to touch me. He made me so sick and nervous. I would cry and beg him not to do it, but he would anyway. I thought after Rozen fooled around with other women and stayed in the bed most of the time with mama, he would have had enough of his pleasures, but the demons in Rozen made him act this way. He would walk around the house naked in front of us girls a lot of times. At night he would come back to the bedroom where the girls were sleeping, pull the covers back, and be standing there naked. He would say, "Would I? In a minute I would." We would be scared to death; be shaking and

Long Walk to Catch the School Bus

shivering so hard that it seemed like every nerve in my body was going to explode. It wrecked my mind and my nerves. I hated him so much because of what he did to me. We would tell mama, but she would brush it off by saying, "Oh, that's just your daddy and he don't mean no harm, he has just been drinking a little bit too much and got confused." I literally couldn't stand her or him, because of those experiences. Mama didn't protect me, and I felt like that was her job to take care of me. She drank and was as bad as he was, just in different ways. That is the reason why I always had mixed feelings toward her because she didn't do me right.

Whenever Rozen would get drunk, it would be the worst. He would cuss, fight and often get the shotgun after mama. They would fight like cats and dogs. We often tried to take the gun away from Rozen so that he wouldn't shoot Mama, but usually whenever he got real mean he would run mama and us kids off from the house. We would jump out of the windows, run to the foot of the hill and get in a ditch to hide out because we knew he would come after us after he finished with mama. We were so scared of his beatings. After things quieted down one of the boys would usually slip back up to the house and peep in the window to see if Rozen had finally passed out from his drinking. Then we could go back into the house. It was a hell right here on earth. These were the worst days of my life. Even though time would pass by, it always seemed to stay the same; it never got any better.

4
Cathouse

The old smokehouse out back of our shabby house was called the "cathouse," it was a gambling hole. A bunch of Rozen and mama's friends would smoke, drink, shoot dice, play poker, and party out there. We kids would slip outside and peep through the cracks in the walls of the smokehouse to see what was going on. I can remember when they would all get drunk. They would be hugging and kissing on whomever and swapping up like a bunch of animals. If we ever said anything about what was going on, mama and Rozen would beat us black and blue and tell us we were supposed to be in the bed asleep. I learned at an early age to keep my mouth shut and do as I was told, or I would suffer the consequences and I knew exactly what that meant.

Rozen had bought a beer joint in town for mama to work in. They finally had moved up a little from the old smokehouse. Rozen still used the cathouse on Sundays because the beer joint was closed. The joint was a little tavern where the drunks came regularly and drank until closing time, which was at midnight. Mama would go to work at about eleven o'clock in the morning and work until midnight. We kids had to stay by ourselves at home and fend for ourselves. Mama was bad about drinking just like Rozen. They were both alcoholics and loved their beer and whiskey. We had to live through this war zone whether we liked it or not; we did not have a choice. It's a shame you can't choose your parents. There is a big difference between people just giving birth to a child and real parents that give love and nourish a child. Believe me, I know.

Rozen would sometimes bring other women home with him at night after he had been out partying; he would make mama get out of bed and cook for them. It did not make any difference what time of night it was, if Rozen said to cook, jump or whatever, mama did it. Most of the time it would be about daybreak when Rozen showed up. Whenever Rozen did bring other women home, mama didn't seem too upset, she always said, "We are all the best of friends, I just want to make Rozen happy." There must have been more to this story than I knew, but I never questioned her, I knew too much already. I never understood why mama loved old Rozen; he was so mean to her and to us kids.

Rozen and mama went to the county sale barn one Tuesday morning. They went there to sell some cows and pigs off the farm and on the way back from the sale barn they stopped and had a few beers somewhere along the way home. Rozen got mad at mama, hit her right square in the nose and she came home with blood just pouring out her nose. My brother took her to the doctor and the doc packed her nose with cotton. Rozen had broken her ribs, blacked both her eyes, pulled her hair out, beat her severely, stomped her several times and mama still kept on drinking and partying with him.

There was a time in the middle of May that Rozen had gotten in a fight in the beer joint over mama. Mr. Woods, the man Rozen got in a fight with, had busted Rozen's face up pretty bad. Mr. Woods broke a beer bottle on Rozen's head and hit him in the face with a barstool. Rozen's face was crushed on one side and his mouth busted up pretty bad also. The doctor had to do surgery, to put his jawbone and mouth back together. I thought, "What a blessing, you are getting what you deserved, it will keep you quiet for a few days." Rozen lay up in bed for about a week after his beating. He made us kids bring him a beer with a straw in it, so he could still have his beer to drink. Nothing ever stopped him from boozing it up. I often wondered if God could hear me because it was so hard living in this house. I just wanted God to get rid of those wild demons in our family. To me we didn't have a home; we had a house full of troubles and heartaches.

July fourth was here and hog killing time on the hill. The boys were getting the hogs ready to put on the pit to cook for Rozen's friends to eat, drink, party and raise cane. They had a big blowout every 4th of July; it's the biggest event of the year. There were so many people I couldn't count them. Thank God it only lasted two days because we kids had to pick up the beer cans and trash after they got through partying.

In the latter part of July, the last Saturday of the month was when we gathered up and went to the Irish picnic in Middle Tennessee. This is like a family reunion where everyone met each year to have a good time and see their old friends they hadn't seen in a while. It was for the old and the young; some drove a long way to get there. They had square dancing and we got to play bingo. There were all kinds of games for the children to play, lots of food to eat and of course plenty of beer to drink or we would not have been going.

Rozen got his old Ford one-ton truck ready for the trip. He puts a tarpaulin up over the back of the sideboards and tied it down tight, so it wouldn't blow off while we are driving down the road. He put two cots (half beds) in the back of the truck for us kids to take a nap, if we got too tired. He put in his keg of beer, some water for us kids in gallon jugs, and a few snacks from the day old bread store for us kids in case we got hungry. Of course the snacks were more than a few days old, because we had gotten them by the truckload to feed our hogs and chickens. They were still fresh to us kids because we hardly ever got sweets to eat anyway. Rozen put in an old slop bucket with a lid on it for us kids to pee-pee in and a few old raggedy chairs for us to sit in. So here we went, we look like the Beverly Hillbillies "from the sticks" going down the road; what a sight it was to see! We kids held on for the ride.

The ride coming back home got really exciting; you can just imagine riding home with Rozen driving, after he had been drinking for about twenty-four hours. We went over the Tennessee River Bridge and Rozen went from one side to the other, scraping the bridge railings with his truck. All of us kids held on tight to each other shouting, "Lord help us." We were afraid Rozen was going to wreck and we would go off into the Tennessee River and drown. On one of the trips across the river, Rozen and mama got in a fight. Mama had taken her best red purse that she had gotten at a yard sale; Rozen grabbed it and threw it out the window into the Tennessee River. We watched it fly by the back of the truck, with mama just cussing a blue streak as it splashed in the water. That trip was always something with our drunken parents. God's hand was always with us kids, or we never would have made it with old Rozen drinking.

In November, a big snow came. Mama and Rozen had gone to town, and we kids knew they wouldn't be in until midnight. Before they left, Rozen said, "Nobody had better get out in the snow!" They had barely gotten to the end of the road when we kids got together and decided to make ourselves some snow cream. We hadn't had a treat in a long time and we were going to take our chances. Dewayne, my brother went outside to get the snow for everyone. We made the snow cream and enjoyed it like we never had anything like it before. While Dewayne was out getting the snow, he got his shoes wet, so we put them under the pot belly wood stove to dry. Everybody went to bed that night and forgot about putting the shoes under the stove. That night when Rozen came in drunk, he saw those shoes under the stove and got us all out of bed. He lined us up, and made everyone of us hold hands together. Rozen took a razor strap off the wall and said, "I am going to beat the hell out of every one of you, until somebody tells me who went out in the d _ _ _ snow." He wasn't sure who went out because we all wore each other's shoes. We all stuck together and weren't going to tell on Dewayne. This is how it always was; we would stick together even if it meant getting a beating. Rozen beat about two or three of us kids and had several yet to go, when

Dewayne stepped up and said, "Daddy, I went out in the snow, please don't whip anyone else, whip me." We all cried hard as Rozen beat Dewayne unmercifully. I mean Rozen beat him until he looked like Jesus being crucified on the cross. Dewayne's back was black and blue; it was awful, blood actually was running down Dewayne's back. The next morning, Dewayne was so sore from the beating he could hardly walk. Mama wouldn't ever do anything to stop Rozen, because he would beat her too. It was a war zone in our own house. We kept it a family secret as much as possible, because Rozen would kill us, if we ever told and he found out.

Rozen started leaving home in the middle of the week, usually about Wednesday afternoon. He was gone and didn't come home, until Saturday mornings. He went to stay with mama's sister, Aunt Renee. They became heavily involved with each other and had a love affair going on that lasted for a year or so. Aunt Renee liked to drink and she knew she could get some of Rozen's money. It was late fall and if we had any kind of crop at all, Rozen would have a little money. We kids farmed the crops, did all the work and then when harvest time came in Rozen got all the money. We hard working kids never got a dime. It didn't make any difference how much money Rozen had we still had to work in the school cafeteria to eat lunch. As usual Rozen spent the money on booze, good times and wild women. I never could understand why Rozen went out with mama's own sister; Aunt Renee was good looking and Rozen's type. It didn't make any difference if they were kinfolk or not, Rozen never culled any woman out. I guess it was all right with mama, because she didn't do anything about it; as soon as Rozen came back home, mama was always glad to be back in his arms. They had a very strange relationship.

In those days when Rozen was gone, we still knew to have our work done or we would catch it when he got back home. He always gave the orders on what was to be done, before he left to go stay a few days with

Aunt Renee. Rozen traded livestock to make money and he usually came out ahead; he just couldn't keep any of it. Rozen made enough money trading and farming for us to live in one of the finest houses comfortably, but we didn't. He foolishly threw it all away.

5
That Stuff Wasn't For Kids

At the age of thirteen, I went to church one Sunday morning with Mrs. Betty Cole. I prayed and asked God to forgive my sins and accepted Jesus Christ into my heart. I knew I had hate in my heart towards my parents, and I had to get it out. I asked God to touch mama and for Rozen to treat us kids right. We were all tired of running and not knowing what we would have to face the next day. I had a headache a lot and I knew it was because of all the fighting. All I could do was just pray.

I came home from church the Sunday morning I got saved, and told Mama I had accepted Jesus into my heart. I wanted her to be proud of me, but she started fussing and telling me I was too young to know about all that stuff. I told her that I knew I was saved, and Jesus was our only hope for our family. About that time, Rozen came in and hit me across the face with his thick calloused hands. It was such a force it made me see stars and made me wet all over myself. Every time I got a whipping, I naturally would wet on myself. Rozen said, "That stuff wasn't for kids, you knew better than to go up in front of that church and talk to that preacher." I thought, "How cruel can this man be!" Rozen whipped me pretty good, but I still prayed to my Heavenly Father everyday and night. I just kept it to myself, because I didn't want to get the razor strap on me.

The Sunday night I was to be baptized in the church, I talked Barbie, my sister-in-law, into taking me to church. I wanted someone to be with me and I knew I could trust her. Barbie was more than a sister-in-law to me; she knew how hard us kids had it and she tried to help us whenever she could, but there was a limit to what she could do.

A lot of times Barbie would take her clothes and alter them a few sizes smaller on the sewing machine, so that us girls could wear them. I knew Rozen and mama did not want me to be baptized that Sunday night, but I trusted God to protect me and went ahead and got baptized anyway. Barbie would never tell on me; she knew I was doing what was right in my heart.

I would be troubled lots of days, and I started reading in my little Bible that Mrs. Betty Cole gave me. I had memorized Psalms 23 and quoted it often to myself. It would give me strength when I was hurting.

The Lord is my shepherd; I shall not want.

He maketh me to lie down in green pastures: he leadeth me beside the still waters.

He restoreth my soul: he leadeth me in the paths of righteousness for his name's sake.

Yea, though I walk through the valley of the shadow of death, I will fear no evil: for thou art with me; thy rod and thy staff, they comfort me.

Thou preparest a table before me in the presence of mine enemies: thou anointest my head with oil; my cup runneth over.

Surely goodness and mercy shall follow me all the days of my life: and I will dwell in the house of the Lord for ever.

(Psalms: 23)

Kat, A Shattered Little Girl

I loved the Lord; I knew He was the only one I could depend on to help me and protect me. At the time I was a child and was being abused, I couldn't understand why God didn't stop it. As I look back, I realize God's hand was on me; things could have been a lot worse and I did plow through it. I came out of it a stronger person.

Mama hurt me by not doing right and protecting me, but I loved her anyway; she was my mama. I could never depend on mama to stand up for me. I really believed she hated herself and me too, but I kept on praying, that mama would find it in her heart to love me. She didn't want me, but I needed her.

6
Sharecropper

In the backyard of our house was another old shack where a sharecropper lived that worked on the farm for Rozen. I was told he had been here for some time. His name was Floyd Edwards. Mr. Edwards was average height, not very heavy at all, his hair was a reddish brown and he had a very loving, quiet, spirit about him. He had a little bit of a limp in his left foot. He told me it was drawn at birth; it was called a clubfoot. Today, I limp like Mr. Edwards did; I also was born with a left foot similar to his. Isn't that odd!

Mr. Edwards seemed to be very close to my mama. They would slip around and be together as much as possible, I had seen them together behind the old shack in the backyard several times, when Rozen wasn't at home. I heard Mr. Edwards tell Mama that he loved her. Late one Sunday night after a crap game at the kitchen table was over and all of the drunks had left, Rozen went to bed and mama was still sitting at the table. Mr. Edwards came into the kitchen and started picking up the beer cans and trash. He never drank or gambled with them that I knew of. He looked around to see if anybody was looking, bent over and kissed mama on the cheek. He sat down with mama at the kitchen table and they started to talk. He said, "When are you going to tell Kathy that I am her daddy," and that's when I found out, that I was the result of their adulterous love affair. Mr. Edwards was telling her that he wanted to tell me that I was his child, but she wanted to wait until I was grown-up. They had a few crosswords. He told mama, he wanted to be a part of my life; it wasn't fair for me not to know he was my real daddy, and he wanted to take me out of the rat hole we were living in. I had always suspected he was my daddy anyway, because Mr. Edwards had always showed me favoritism over the other children. When Mr. Edwards helped us chop cotton in the field, he would help me get my row out and help me catch up, when I got behind. There was one time he brought a sack of jawbreakers from the store, passed out one to each of the other kids and gave me all that was left. That put a smile on my face.

One summer Saturday afternoon, Mr. Edwards and I were sitting on the front porch, while mama and Rozen were in town at the beer joint. He said to me, "I want to tell you something child, but you've got to promise, you won't tell anyone else." He said, "Your mama and I have been involved for sometime; that's why I stay up here on this hill to be with her and you. You are my daughter; I helped deliver you in the back of an old station wagon on the way to the hospital. Your mama was in labor and she couldn't wait until we got to the hospital." I said to him, "Where was Rozen when all of this was going on?" Mr. Edwards said, "Rozen was out on the town as usual. So I was the first one to see you, when you came naked into this world. You are my little girl. I have wanted to tell you for a long time, but your mama said it would only cause trouble by you, Kathy, knowing the truth. Your mama is afraid it will wreck your life and cause you to hate her forever." I wasn't really surprised, but it gave me lots of answers why mama and Rozen treated me different from the other kids. There was a deep hurt within that stabbed me like a knife. I wondered sometimes just who I really was, or if anyone wanted me. I was raised in this big family, but I always felt empty and all alone, I always knew I was different in lots of ways from the other kids. I told Mr. Edwards that I felt like it wrecked mama's life instead of mine, because she is the one that shows so much hate towards me. I think sometimes mama can't stand herself or me either; hopefully it's just that every time she looks at me, she is reminded of my real daddy, Mr. Floyd Edwards. So I just pray, that some day mama will face the truth about the past, and let me know that she really loves me. I can honestly say, I am proud to know for sure that old Rozen wasn't my daddy; I heard it right out of mama's mouth that Sunday night and then later from Mr. Edwards's own mouth. Rozen wasn't ever fit to be called daddy, and that is why I always had called him, "Rozen."

Mr. Edwards was helping me wash the dishes one night, after he had told me I was his daughter. He told me he loved me very much, and he wished things could be different on the hill. Mr. Edwards said, "I know Rozen is mean to you kids, but I can not do one thing about it! Rozen will kill your Mama if he ever catches us together; it is a bad situation between us up here on this hill and I am right here in the middle of it all. I guess I will stay out back in the old shack until Rozen runs me off. I don't really have any place to go and very little money, but I will stay as long as I can." I felt sorry for him; he really didn't have any choice but to stay in the confusion, if he wanted to be near mama and me.

I never felt any love from mama or Rozen. I grew up as a child always believing in my heart, Mr. Floyd Edwards was my daddy. After a few months had passed, I told Mama that Mr. Edwards told me he was my daddy. She cussed me, kicked me real hard in the butt, and told me that Rozen would beat her if anyone ever found out. I know she was trying to scare me, because she was guilty as sin. I thought that was the reason why she hated me so much, I knew the truth. Mama was mean and hateful to me. I begged mama to love me so many times. I tried to be a good little girl but nothing pleased her, I was just another brat to her. I wanted to feel loved so much by her, that I would do anything to get her to be nice to me. I just couldn't understand why I was the ugly duckling and the one picked on all the time. I overlooked her doing wrong; I just wanted mama's love. I wanted her to treat me as well as she treated the other kids. She wasn't mean to the other girls, and that's why I knew she hated me so much. My hurt was so deep that I can not begin to explain it. I can remember mama would grab my nappy hair, twist it around her hand, then yank it hard and kick me in the butt. Mama's favorite statement was, "I brought you in this world and I can take you out! Do you hear me?" Her words were so harsh, believe me, I did hear her and I knew she meant business!

All of the other kids on the hill had heard Rozen and mama arguing about me being Mr. Edwards' daughter and it kept things in an uproar. They would say, "Rozen is going to beat the crap out of you, because you think that you are not his." It kept me upset, and I knew that I was the black sheep of the family, but I still loved my brothers and sisters. They were right, Rozen did beat me pretty good, because mama got to drinking and told him that Mr. Edwards and I had been talking. After Rozen got through whipping me, he ran Mr. Edwards off of the hill without me even getting to say, "Good bye." My heart was shattered to pieces that day; that was the last time I saw my daddy; I cried silently and prayed daily, that I would get to see him just one more time before I see him in heaven. I always kept the fact that he was my daddy, in my heart and never ever discussed it any more to anyone. I was just a kid fighting for existence.

7
Hole In The Wall

The gambling, drinking and hell raising continued on the hill. Rozen started to teaching the boys how to shoot dice, gamble and sell beer. He said they had to learn from somewhere. Mama kept on drinking and working some at the beer joint. She slowed down a little after she started getting morning sickness again, we all knew what this meant, another baby to wash diapers for. It seemed we never did get out of washing baby bottles and those nasty diapers.

Mama took me to the dentist because I had a toothache for several days and I had a swollen jaw. Mama left me at the dentist office about ten o'clock and told me to walk down the street to the beer joint called the "Hole In The Wall," when I got finished. Mama wanted to go have a few beers with her friends while she waited on me to get through at the dentist. The dentist couldn't pull my tooth because it was abscessed. He rubbed some kind of gel on my gums to help stop the pain, gave me some medicine and told me to come back when the infection was gone. I walked down to the old beer joint where mama was, and she was already "two sheets in the wind," if you know what I mean. She wasn't ready to go home yet, so I had to sit up there on a barstool with her and waited until she got ready to go home. It was getting nighttime and I never dreamed of being in a beer joint all day sick with a toothache.

There was a man named Harry Sawyer that had been coming to the hill to gamble with Rozen; he comes in and sits down on the barstool beside me and buys me a RC cola. It was hot that day and I was wearing a white sleeveless tank top with a pair of faded out cut off jeans and a pair of ragged shoes. I was poor and ragged looking and I don't want to be bragging, but I had been told I was a knockout. I was developing very well at the age of fifteen and I could have passed easily for eighteen if I had the right clothes. Harry looked at mama and saw that she was in bad shape and I mean bad shape. She had a little bit too much to drink. He said, "Mrs. Telson, I will be glad to take you and your daughter home, it don't look like you are in any shape to drive." She refused his offer and said she was going to stay until closing time, but asked Harry to take me home instead. He replied, "I'll be more than glad to," with a smile from ear to ear.

We went and got into his orange convertible car; he drove toward home and about a half mile from the house he stopped at the curve in the road where the hog pen was. He put his arm up over the back of the seat, looked at me and said, "You sure are a pretty thing." I got a little nervous and I said, "Thank you." Well before I knew it he laid a big kiss on me. I pushed him away and said, "I'd better get to the house." I did have a toothache. He took me to the house and told me, "I didn't mean to scare you, I really do like you." I just said, "OK."

8
Sold For A Sack Of Potatoes

Harry worked for a produce company, and he started bringing hundred pound sacks of potatoes and onions for the family because he was interested in me. He felt if he could buy his way in, then Rozen would allow him to date me. I always felt like he was trying to buy me for hundred pound sack of potatoes and onions. At this time he jokingly told me he was going to buy me off of Telson Hill. He was kind and gentle to me in the beginning. I was fifteen and he was twenty-four, when Rozen allowed us to start seeing each other. I never got to go out with Harry by myself at the beginning. All we got to do was sit in the living room or out under the shade tree and talk. Sometimes we would sit in his convertible car and listen to the radio.

Eventually mama and Rozen would let us go to the local dairy bar, but would always send one of the other kids with us. They were eager to go because that was the only time they got a dairy treat. There were a few times that I got to go to his mother's house and grill out. Harry was beginning to tell me that he thought he loved me, and I was thinking that anything would beat the "hell hole" I was living in at home. Mama and Rozen were starting to let me date him more regularly, and Harry kept bringing the hundred pound sacks of produce. He had to bring big quantities because there were so many of us to feed and this always made Rozen happy.

Harry had really gotten in thick with Rozen, bringing him beer and buttering him up because Harry was getting serious about me. He was coming almost every night to the hill to see me. Believe me, it was starting to cost him big time. He said, 'I love you and I don't care what price I have to pay, but I am going to have you one way or the other." It made me feel good because then I believed he really loved me, it sounded bad that he had to pay for me, but at least someone did care for me. Harry was off from work every Tuesday and I skipped school one Tuesday to go off and be with him. I rode the bus to school with all of the other kids; I went in the front door of the school and then straight out the back door where Harry was waiting for me. We spent the day together planning on getting married real soon. He said that we could live with his mama and daddy; they were good people and would help us out. It sounded good to me.

I knew Harry acted a little different from the average person and seemed a little jealous of me. He told me not to be flirting with any boys at school. I thought that was silly because no one ever looked at me anyway. I really did love Harry at fifteen years old. I was hoping and praying for a good life with him, He was the first person except for my real daddy that ever showed me a little kindness. I willingly got heavily involved with Harry to get away from the mad house I was living in. I felt like I was a poor, ragged, crippled, ugly girl that nobody would ever want, and I had better get out while I had the chance.

Harry gave me his graduation picture, and I kept it hid in my school notebook. I would look at his picture, rub my hands over the face of the picture and pray that Harry was real. I believed what he was telling me was true. I wanted a good home so badly and I wanted to feel the love that had been missing in my life. He would take his hand, rub it through my long silky auburn hair, stroke it gently and tell me how pretty I was. He would look into my big green eyes and say, "We are going to have a good life together, I promise." Harry's words were so convincing that I felt in my heart it was going to be forever and ever. He was my charming prince that rode onto Telson Hill in an orange convertible to rescue this poor ragged girl that no one wanted. I loved him very deeply. I will never forget July 4, 1971. There was a big barbecue outside that night with a hog cooking on the pit. There were about twenty-five drunks out there, drinking and gambling. Harry came to be with me, but I was working in the kitchen most of the time. Harry and I wanted to get married, but Mama and Rozen wouldn't allow it. I think it was because they knew they could get more work out of me or get more produce out of Harry. About two o'clock that Sunday morning, while Mama and Rozen were drunk with all their friends out in the "cathouse," I slipped out the window to meet Harry at the foot of the hill. I had already packed a few clothes in a brown paper sack, and Harry had put them in the trunk of his car when no one was looking. He told me to be ready to get off the hill; we were going to elope that night to Florence, Alabama to get married. I was scared to death, but we loved each other. I knew Harry was going to be strict on me and jealous, but it didn't matter to me because I wanted to have a home. I felt like Harry loved me, and I thought being married could in no way be as bad as Telson Hill. I believed our love was forever.

We drove the rest of the night and arrived in Florence early in the morning. We went to get something to eat while we were waiting for the courthouse to open at nine o'clock. We finished eating breakfast and went to the courthouse. We wanted to be the first ones there when they opened the doors. We realized nothing was open on this Monday because of the holiday falling on Sunday. So we had to find us a place to stay that night until the next morning when the courthouse would be open. That next morning we went to the county courthouse to get married. They asked for some identification from me and I didn't have any. I was fifteen and I didn't know about that stuff, I didn't even know what an "ID" was. Harry looked at me and said, "It looks like we got a problem." I said, "Well why didn't you tell me I needed something called an ID, you know I don't know nothing, I'm green as a gourd." The clerk looked at both of us and thought, "What have I got here?" They wanted to know my age and I said, "I will be sixteen in ten days." Harry started shaking his head and handed her his ID. He was about to get upset at the lady.

He had heard that you could get married at fifteen in Florence and that's why we went down there. The clerk told us that I was under age and that I needed someone to sign for me. I say, "Well, can I go out on the street and get somebody that is old enough, I can't go back home, they will beat me to death?" She said, "No honey, I'm sorry, you have to have your parents sign for you." Harry told her, "You don't understand, we have to get married, her parents are drunks, they will shoot the h _ _ _ out of both of us! Her daddy is a mean man." The clerk said, "I can't break the rules, you need a guardian." Harry said, "Let's get out of here."

Harry found a cheap motel and we started making some phone calls to a Mississippi courthouse. They gave us the same answer as we had already heard. I was literally scared to death to go back home, and Harry was scared Rozen would have him put in jail for fooling with a minor. We didn't know what to do but to stay there for a few days. I knew it was wrong and the guilt was starting to set in, I had always tried to be a good girl, but now I am making a mistake that will go with me to my grave. I was so desperate to get away from home that I guess I would have done almost anything. It was sad to be in that kind of situation, but that is just how it actually was.

I didn't know much about Harry except he came from a good family and had been kind to me the few months I had known him. I had run away from home with Harry thinking I was going to make myself a new life. Here I am, can't get married and can't go back home to a mama that would protect me. You can imagine what was about to happen to me. It's hard to explain, but it's the truth; I experienced things that I had never even considered happening to me. I had never been with him sexually and now here I was at his mercy and Harry was ready for his needs to be fulfilled. When I left home I thought we would be married by now; I couldn't ask for any pity because I had gotten myself into this predicament and it was a big mess. I had made my bed hard, and now I had to lay in it. I had to take the consequences. It was painful, because it was not the right thing to do and the guilt was starting to tear me apart. I knew I was doing wrong; I closed my eyes, grit my teeth, tried to put my mind to it and did what was expected of me. I blame only myself, so I alone have to deal with the guilt. I am so ashamed, but I hated home so badly. I knew this was the wrong way out, but it was too late to back out now and it did get me away from the childhood trauma of Telson Hill. Well, believe me, I was about to start a journey that in my wildest imagination, I could have never dreamed.

After about three days, we started to run out of money; so, scared to death, we decided to go back to Telson Hill. As we were driving up the road to the hill, I thought, would Mama and Rozen be drunk? I thought Harry was going to put me out and leave me back on the hill. I talked him into staying there with me until Rozen came home. Mama cussed and raved so loud almost bursting our eardrums. When Rozen came in, he cussed and threatened us too, and we thought he might go get his gun. He told Harry, "Hell, yes, you are going to marry her, cause she is probably knocked up with your baby." Harry said, "I love her, I want to marry her and take care of her." So, Harry, Mama, Rozen and myself went down to the county courthouse to get married. By this time they were ready to get rid of me and sign for me to get married. What a wedding day to remember, July 13, 1971!

On the way home, Rozen wanted to stop and get some beer to drink. So, when we stopped at the store, Harry went inside to get a six-pack for them while I waited in the car with Mama and Rozen. I didn't want Harry to leave me alone with those two, because I knew that I was going to catch a good cussing. Rozen cussed me and told me what a tramp I was for running off with Harry. He said, "You are no good for nothing. I should have just beat the h _ _ _ out of you and shot him." I was really getting nervous, I couldn't wait to get them back on the hill and put them out. I left that day and didn't see my family for several months.

9
From The Frying Pan Into The Fire

We drove to Harry's parents and moved into the downstairs bedroom. His parents hugged me and welcomed me to the family. I apologized for worrying Mrs. Sawyer while Harry and I were in Alabama. So I was married now and starting a brand new life. I was happy to have a real family that loved me and wanted me.

Life was much better, so much better than where I came from. Harry's parents were good Christian people. His mother was so good to me; she was always cooking and trying to make me feel cared for. I asked if it was all right for me to call her, "Mama Sawyer." She said, "Child you can call me anything you want to." She knew I had a hard childhood and went out of her way to welcome me into their home. Mama Sawyer sewed a lot, she would buy pretty material and make me clothes. That was special treatment because I wasn't so ragged looking now. With new clothes I looked much better. Harry took me to town, bought me some good underclothes and new shoes. Harry had a bunch of quarters saved up in a gallon fruit jar and bought me some wedding rings that cost $43.00. He was good in lots of ways in the beginning, but he wouldn't go to church, so I went with his mom and dad. I had always gone to church with Mrs. Betty Cole, and I knew that was where I was supposed to be on Sundays. I had done wrong by running off with Harry and I wanted to get my life straightened out, so I knew the first step was to repent for my sins and get in church. We were married about two weeks when Harry started going out to the poolroom; he didn't drink, so I didn't worry. I never said anything because I had a good roof over my head, plenty to eat, pretty homemade clothes and I felt safe with his parents. I always enjoyed my times talking with Mama Sawyer; she was so good to talk with. I loved her very much and I felt good when I was with her, because she would always listen to me. Grandpa Sawyer would stay with us often; his wife had passed away when Harry and I were dating. I became a real close buddy with grandpa and I always enjoyed his funny jokes. Grandpa was in fairly good health and had a lot of humor in him to be eighty years old.

Six months passed, Harry and I rented a little house for $45 a month. I had finally gotten my first house with Harry and was enjoying fixing it up. I was really trying to have me a pretty home and getting ready for my new baby. Mrs. Betty Cole, the lady that had taught me in Sunday school, had given me a baby shower. My church friends were always so good to me and they had given me a lot of nice things for the baby including a baby bassinet. I always felt loved by the ladies from my hometown church.

Harry had hit me a few times, so I knew that he had a temper and I needed to handle him with gloves on. The first time Harry whipped me, he took his belt off and used it on me. I made him mad about something, I can't remember why. I never complained about the way he treated me, I took it, because I didn't want to make him angry. One day after he left to go to work, I wanted to change the way the furniture was arranged, so I spent the day changing the house around and cooking him a good hot supper.

Although Harry was sometimes violent, I wanted to try to make him happy. I was thankful to have a home and only one person to abuse me instead of several, as was the case in my dysfunctional childhood home. When Harry came in that night from work, I met him at the door with a hug. As soon as he saw the changes I had made in the house, he shoved me across the room and started cussing. He was mad because I had moved the furniture around without asking his permission. He pushed the couch from one side of the room to the other side where it originally was. He scared me the way he was acting. He threw me up against the wall and started hitting me on my shoulders with his fists and yanking my long hair. I hated having long hair because it got yanked all the time, but Harry would not let me cut it. I realized then that I had gone from the frying pan into the fire. I couldn't believe I was in the same situation that caused me to leave when I was back home. We had been married for eight and a half months, and I was eight months pregnant. I didn't have a mama or daddy to go home to because they were as bad as he was. I was sixteen years old, so all I could do was take it and hope things would get better, but life seemed to stand still.

We had neighbors, but we never socialized with them, everyone knew Harry was very particular and had a smart mouth on him. The first week we lived there I was outside hanging out clothes and he came running out to where I was and started cussing at me about something. Some of the neighbors were in their backyard and they could see and hear him raving like a wild animal. No one wanted trouble with him so they kept their distance. They all knew he was a strange character and felt sorry for his dogs and me.

I remember one time when he bought a riding lawn mower. We were still living in the little $45 rental house. We didn't have an outbuilding, so he put the mower in the backyard, in the dog pin with his two German Shepherds. He didn't want anyone getting on his mower, so he locked the gate and put the key in his pocket. I knew better than to touch it, and everyone else did too. The neighbors and I knew not to mess with him or his stuff. He even had the children in the neighborhood scared to walk across our yard. He had yelled at them one time and that is all it took.

One day Harry came in mad after feeding his dogs. I didn't feed them because I wasn't allowed to bother his dogs, his mower or anything else he had. He came in and threw me up against the kitchen wall. He was hitting me on the shoulders and slapping my face. I was hollering, "Please don't hit me, you're going to make me lose the baby." He whipped me because the dogs had eaten the leather and foam off of the lawnmower seat; they had chewed the seat down to the chrome. Harry was cussing me like I was one of his dogs. I told him I couldn't help it. First of all, I didn't have the key to get in the dog pen and secondly I wasn't allowed to go in the pen. He said it was my fault because I let it happen. He would get mad for no reason and blame everything on me. I laid in bed for a few days after that episode with my feet propped up on a pillow because I began to spot some blood.

Harry kept me nervous and tore up most of the time. I went to Dr. Jones, lied and said that I had fallen, because I didn't want the doctor to know Harry had been acting crazy. That night I was up most of the time with stomach cramps. Early the next morning Harry took me to the hospital because I was in so much pain. I was so concerned there might be something wrong with my baby, but it was time for him to come. I was in labor all that day, that night and most of the next day. I was in so much pain they finally had to use forceps to take him from me. I had been in labor for thirty-six hours and had hemorrhaged so bad they gave me blood. I was so exhausted from giving birth to a nine pound, seven ounce baby boy. I thought, "I never want to go through anything like this again," but we pulled through it, both my new son, Jeff and me. He had a head full of dark hair; he was such a cute baby. He was in good health, considering what we had been through. I just wish Harry could have been proud of our new son like I was.

Harry was really upset because I was in the hospital for so long, he didn't have any insurance and knew he would have to pay for it out of his own pocket. I had been there a few days when he came in and said, "You're going home, I don't care about these doctors or nurses, you're going home. You can lay in the bed at home with your feet propped up." He went to the nurse's station and told them, "I can't pay this hospital bill, she is going home!" The nurses told him I couldn't leave because the doctors had not released me. After he finished his "fit with the nurses," they got a wheelchair, put me in it, brought the baby to me and wheeled me to Harry's car. I went home and laid in bed with my feet propped up for several days.

Sharon, one of my sisters, came to take care of me because I was so weak. I should have still been in the hospital, but what Harry said, went. I was at my roads end, mentally and physically because of the difficult labor and from the beatings. I thought, "Dear God, am I going to be strong enough to pull through this?" My sister stayed with me for a week and then one of Harry's sisters came and stayed a few days. Finally after about ten days, I was up on my feet trying to take care of my new baby and myself. I loved my new son, Jeff, with all my heart, and clung to him; we didn't have anyone else.

Harry was gambling and staying out all night. He loved to play cards and shoot pool. Sometimes he would be gone two or three days at a time. I never knew when Harry was coming home. He hardly ever came straight home after work. I didn't have a phone, a car, money or anything. He would do anything he wanted to me, and he tried to make me like it. I couldn't understand why Harry acted this way. I was good to him; I cooked, washed and ironed his clothes, loved him and never talked back. It seemed Harry enjoyed knocking me around. I thought, "What have I done to deserve this?"

I remember a time he hit me in the face; he damaged my nose and blacked my eye. He would hit me several times with his fist, grab my hair and trip me with his legs. Then he would just stomp me with his shoes. I was so scared that I didn't know what to do. I prayed, "Oh, God, make a way for me to get out of this." My family wouldn't help me because they didn't want to get involved, and Harry would threaten anyone else who tried to help me. I would go out into the woods, sit on a stump and cry out to God, believing that some day it would be better.

At this time in my life, I felt Harry really didn't love me. I thought,

"Am I not pretty enough, what is it?" I had always tried to keep myself neat, and I wasn't overweight; I weighed 110 pounds at 5'9." I knew I wasn't a Miss America, but I didn't look like a dog either. I just couldn't feel good about myself; I was so used to being beaten down all the time from Harry. I had always wanted to feel loved, I never felt it at home with mama and Rozen, and now not even with Harry. So I lived with all my hurt and pain and tried to concentrate on raising my son. Jeff was my life. I loved and adored my baby, and did everything to be a good mother. It was Jeff and myself, alone in this cruel world. I was determined to make my marriage work.

I prayed daily to the Lord as I knew He was my only hope. I got so close to the Lord I felt I could reach out and touch Him. I knew his spirit was always with me. I know God never promised me a life free of sorrow and pain, just that He would always walk with me and give me the strength to survive.

After Harry would come back from those three or four days of laying out, he would be tired, cranky, ill and of course cussing. He'd say that he had slept in the truck instead of driving the two miles home from the produce plant. Several times the police woke Harry up while he was sleeping in his truck. They wanted to see if anything was wrong. He'd sleep in the truck or he'd sleep somewhere else. I often wondered why he would sleep in his old truck instead of coming home to a warm and clean house. I always had his supper cooked and sitting on the stove waiting on him regardless what hour of the night he came in. Harry was a very unpredictable person; you never knew what mood he would come home in. I couldn't understand it; Harry didn't drink or do drugs, so I didn't know what his problem was.

He beat me so much that I didn't care about him being gone anyway. I always dreaded seeing him come home; I didn't want to have anything to do with him. He'd say, "I will _ _ _ _ you anytime I want to. You are my wife and you'll do as I say." He'd beat me and then force himself on me. I hated living with him this way. It just seemed like I was in prison. Back home was bad enough, but here I was in my second hell, and all I had was my little baby boy. Harry never gave me money for my personal needs. My sister, Sharon, took me to the health department so I could get some birth control pills; I knew I didn't want to wind up with another baby by this animal. I'd been through one war during my childhood, and here I was again, in the second battlefield. It made me tough as nails, and I was determined that I was going to make it and be somebody. I kept praying for strength to leave and walk away.

10
Be Quiet, Dogs!

It was a cold night in October, and I had a cast on my leg from foot surgery. The doctors operated on my bad foot and cut the ankle cord in an attempt to help me stop walking with a limp. It hurt a little but I wouldn't complain; I was thankful I had one good foot to walk on. I realized it could be worse. Harry was fussing about something as usual and I knew I was probably going to get a whipping. He was crazy whenever he got mad and I did not want him to hurt me with that cast on my leg.

About nine o'clock there was a knock at the door, so Harry went to the door. A man had come to the door to talk to Harry about his old forty-model ford car that was in our front yard for sale. While Harry was at the front door, I left and went out the back door to get away from him. I was going to a neighbor's house to call my brother, Dewayne, to come after me. I went hopping out the back door on one leg, dragging the other leg with the cast on it. I got a piece away from the house and the neighbor's dogs started barking at me. I was down in the ditch trying to crawl on my knees because I didn't want Harry to be able to see me. Crawling was difficult with a cast up to my knee. I was trying to keep the dogs quiet because I was afraid Harry would hear them and know where I was. Sure enough, the old dogs kept barking. Well, Harry found me missing in the house and followed the barking dogs. Harry caught me just as I was about to get in the neighbor's yard.

He grabbed me by the hair of my head, kicked my good leg out from under me and dragged me back to the house. He pushed me down in the front yard and started stomping me with his big number twelve foot. After he was through stomping me in the back, he picked me up and threw me on the front porch just like I was his dog. I lay there for a while because I couldn't move. He beat me just about unconscious that time. He said, "I'll teach you a lesson about running off, I am the d _ _ _ boss around here and you do as I say! Do you hear me?" I could barely get the words out of my mouth, because I was in so much pain, but I managed to say, "Yes, sir! You are the boss." I never fussed or talked back to him; I knew better.

After I laid there on the porch for a while, I tried to crawl inside the house. I could hardly move because I was hurting so badly. I finally got back inside the house and crawled to the bedroom. I pulled myself up on the bed. I tried to pull a pillow up under my left leg, the one with the cast on it, to elevate my leg because it was throbbing so much. He hurt me pretty bad this time.

My cast had a crack in it from the stomping. Harry came in the bedroom the next day and said, "You should've known better. You just have to learn not to disobey me." He kissed me and acted like it never happened. Each day I laid in the bed, Harry would tell me it was my fault. After I recovered a little from the beating I went back to the doctor and had my cast redone. This caused me not to heal as quickly. I was twenty-one years old when this happened.

I just wondered sometimes if I had done something that caused Harry to be the way he was. I wished I knew why he hated me so much; I always was good to him. My mind was so battered that I didn't know if I was mentally sick like him. I was too scared to do anything; I was afraid to stay and afraid to go. I got in trouble regardless of what I did. The only time he ever told me he loved me was on our wedding day. He said, "I won't tell you again that I love you, it sticks until I tell you different. It's nonsense to repeat it over and over." That was just the way Harry was.

He bought me a new set of wedding rings with diamonds shortly after the beating. I now had a diamond ring on my finger, but I didn't care if it had been a string around my finger. Harry must have been feeling a little guilty about beating me and probably that is why I got the new rings. I believe it was a little late to think a ring would make me feel any better. What I really had was a "rope" around my neck. My body still ached and I was so sore and bruised for days. It took a good while to get over this one. I didn't ever want anything from him except some respect and kindness. He made me feel ugly and cheap like I was no better than the hogs in his hog pen. He cussed me so much that I actually felt like his dog.

Harry would grab my hair, shove me in front of the mirror and say, "Look at you. You are nothing but a cripple, ugly, son of a b _ _ _ _! You are lucky to have me. I bought you off of Telson Hill. You are not worth the salt that goes in your bread." He was always bringing up the fact that I was a cripple because of my deformed foot. Harry told me what he thought of me very often and believe me, it sank deep into my heart. I always thought, "If this is love, then I don't know what hate is."

I wasn't that ugly or that bad of a person. I believe now as I look back on all of the abuse Harry dished out to me, it was all because he was insanely jealous. I really believe he had a split personality, He would be good one minute and a devil the next. I kept myself clean and wore my best rags that I had gotten at the yard sales on Saturday mornings. I thought it was my fault why Harry couldn't love me. I will have to say I failed him in one area of our marriage. I never wanted anything to do with him sexually. If Harry just had some patience with me and loved me a little, I believe I could have overcome the pain from the past and been the wife that he needed. I was totally numb in this area of our marriage and I couldn't help that I was like a dead woman still alive. By Harry battering me physically and mentally, he reinforced the pain from my childhood trauma. But he just buried it in me a little deeper. Harry didn't know how to love me or himself either; he was just a cold lost man full of hate. Something must have happened to him in his earlier years to have so much bitterness and anger in him.

I wondered some days what it would feel like to have a normal husband to care for me, love me, and hold me. I dreamed of having good smelling cologne, a new outfit that didn't come from a yard sale, a good T-bone steak, a man to pray with me and go to church with me and a husband that enjoyed socializing just a little with friends. I couldn't imagine life ever being this way with Harry. We had no kind of life at all as a married couple. I ached to be loved by him the right way in God's eyes, but all I could do was hope and try to survive in Harry's cold cruel world. I tried to do the right thing by staying, but I was only in his way.

11
Good Old Maverick

Time had passed and we had moved to a small country community called Birch Leaf. We were about six miles from town and two miles from the local country grocery store. I always enjoyed walking, so I walked beside the road to the little grocery store whenever Harry would give me permission. We had a little farm with five acres of land, a two-bedroom brick house, a small barn, a little garden and some hogs that Harry had raised. Harry always enjoyed working in the garden and he had a pepper patch, because he could sell the peppers on his produce route.

Harry had his faults, but one thing I could say good about Harry, he was an extremely hard worker. He worked hard, sick or well; I never knew of him ever missing a days work. If he had worked as hard toward our marriage as he worked in general, we would have had a good marriage. I desperately wanted our marriage to have love and happiness.

My neighbor across the road was Mrs. Modean Williams. She was a very kind, caring and loving older lady. She was married to a Baptist minister and they were good Christian people. I was afraid to talk very much to them, because I was ashamed of them finding out about Harry and myself. They soon realized that Harry was a peculiar type of person, and knew they had to be careful how they treated their odd neighbors. It was obvious the Williams suspected what was going on in our household. I didn't tell them, but they could tell that I acted distant. Their daughter had previously been acquainted with Harry and knew he was different. But, Mrs. Modean still visited and tried to be a good neighbor to us. Mrs. Modean invited Jeff to come over and play with her grandchildren who lived next door to her. Her grandchildren were about Jeff's age and they wanted someone to play with. They took up with Jeff, our son, and gradually I was able to feel comfortable with her as a friend. Fortunately, Harry didn't seem to mind that Jeff and I had become such good friends with our neighbors.

I didn't have any way to get to church since Harry didn't go, so Mrs. Modean invited Jeff and me to ride to church with her and Brother Williams, her husband. I always looked forward to going to church with them, because I not only needed all the spiritual help I could get, I just needed to get out of the house. This is one of the few things that I did have permission to do, go to church. I believed in God, and He was my strength. I usually went with the Williams to church on Sunday nights and not on Sunday mornings. I didn't like going to the morning services because I didn't like people asking me questions like, "Well, where is your husband today?" I was ashamed and didn't want to explain why Harry didn't want to go to church. I was a very private person and I didn't want to get close to anybody.

My son was now old enough to start Kindergarten. Jeff was very excited about riding the big yellow school bus and having some new playmates. I had already taught Jeff his colors and how to count to a hundred. He was a good kid and I was very proud of him. The first day that I put him on the bus to go to school, I stood with him out in the driveway beside the road while he waited for the big yellow bus to come. I looked Jeff over good to make sure that his new bright yellow shirt was tucked into his new blue jeans. He looked so good. When I saw the bus coming, I started to cry because my baby was leaving me. It was harder on me that it was on him. He gave me a big hug and said, "Mama, I will be alright, I am going to have a big time." He was just so excited to get to go somewhere.

I sadly walked back to the empty house and realized my baby was growing up. Jeff was my life and I was going to be lost with him gone, because he and I were always together. We had been so close, because for most of his life we only had each other. Jeff was always under my heels; every step I took, he took one too.

I wanted to go to work so badly and I told Harry that if I could just go to work I would give him my paycheck. I needed to make some money to buy my personal stuff and I wanted to meet people. I needed some friends. Mrs. Modean got me my first job at a little plant called HIS in the next little town. It was a factory for making blue jeans. My first job at the plant was putting grippers on the top of the blue jeans. I thought it was an easy job, but I had to be careful and not put my finger under the machine guard because I didn't want a gripper hole in my finger. My son started school one day, and the next day I started to work. This worked out very well because by working I never got lonesome due to Jeff starting to school. I started out making $1.95 an hour, which was a lot to me since I didn't have a quarter to my name. I worked hard to make myself a good employee and always volunteered for overtime because I always needed the extra money. The plant was about five miles from the house and I would pay five dollars a week to ride to work with my neighbors and a dollar a day for after school care for my son. Jeff would ride the bus and get off down the road at a neighbor's house, Mrs. Neal's. She was keeping him after school. I took about five dollars a week from my check to eat on, and the rest went for bills. Working helped me forget what was happening at home. I just lived in my own little world. I was working to help Harry pay bills, and still trying to be a good mother to my son and keep the home together.

Harry never went to any of Jeff's school activities or showed any interest in him whatsoever. Therefore, I didn't get to go to any of the school functions either, because I didn't have a way to go. I started praying that Harry would let me have a car. I had worked at the plant for six months and felt that I could pay for my own car. I wanted to have a car so I could have a way to church, to work, to Jeff's schoolhouse and to the grocery store. These were the only four places that I had any business going, and I would feel lucky just to have permission to go to them. I had depended on the neighbors for too long and I just started praying that it would be okay with Harry for me to get a car. I believed that I could make the payment, but I had never done any banking business, such as having a checking account or borrowing any money. I knew that I could learn to drive if my husband would give me permission. I didn't know how to drive, but I was eager to learn.

While I was at work, one of my sister-in-laws told me about her daddy having a car for sale. I came home from work that day and told Harry about it when he came home. He said, "I am not going to have anything to do with it; if you think you are capable of getting a car, you just get it. Who do you think is going to let you borrow money to buy a car? You can't drive, you don't have no money, you don't have no bank account and you don't have no credit. You have been working at that little old penniless job for only a few months. You have got to be crazy to even think about somebody letting you borrow money. You don't even have any drivers license to drive." Harry just didn't think I could do it, but I was still believing in God for a miracle. The Man upstairs was watching over me and I just had enough faith that I could get the car.

The next day on my lunch hour, I walked from the factory uptown to the bank and asked to talk to someone about borrowing some money for a car. The man I asked said, "I am the man." His name was George and he was the loan officer. I told him I had been working at the HIS plant for six months and hadn't missed a day's work. I wanted to borrow money to buy a car. I told him that I had found a yellow 64 Maverick car that was in good condition except the heater didn't work very well. He laughed and said, "That won't cost but about five dollars to get fixed; that sounds like a thermostat." That didn't matter to me, because I could always just put on more clothes and put a blanket around Jeff until I could afford to fix the heater. Five dollars was a lot of money to me.

My sister-in-law's daddy, Mr. Pounds, was moving out of the state and he was the one selling the car. George let me borrow the $500 dollars for the car and Mr. Pounds met George and me the next day at the bank to finalize the sale. I knew that it was the power of God that touched George's heart to let me have the money for the car. He took a chance on me because he didn't know me from Adam. I was so thankful that he had faith in me and gave me a chance to build myself up some credit without asking a lot of questions. The average person would have never been so compassionate, but George saw something in me. God was obviously in control of this business deal.

I bought the 64 Maverick for $500 and paid $45 a month for a year until it was paid back. I told George and Mr. Pounds that I didn't know how to drive the car, so Mr. Pounds drove it to my house and put it in my driveway. When I got home from work that day, my husband wasn't home yet. I got into my car and just prayed over the steering wheel saying, "Lord, give me the knowledge to drive this car, and don't let Harry beat me tonight for having it." Again, I felt like God had answered another prayer for me.

I started the car, put it in drive, and pulled it out into the back pasture behind the barn. I rode around in circles while Jeff sat at the barn on a bucket watching me. I was afraid for him to ride with me. I would put it in drive; go for a piece, put on the brake and almost throw myself through the windshield. I would stop, pray for a while and then put it in reverse, look back until I felt I was going to break my neck and mash the gas. I barely missed the telephone pole in the middle of the field. Then, I would go forward again. After about an hour, I parked my yellow Maverick in the field behind the old hog barn. I knew I had to tell Harry before he saw it. He was going to be in shock whenever I tell him about the car.

When Harry came home from work that night, as I saw him driving up in the driveway, I started getting nervous. When he walked in the door, I went up to Harry and gave him a big hug as I usually tried to do every day. He was mean to me, but I still loved him and would always meet him at the door with a kiss. Some days he would accept me, and some days he would be ill and say, "I didn't eat your breakfast," and push me away. He just didn't want me touching him sometimes, but thank the Lord; tonight he was in fairly good shape.

I decided to go on and tell Harry about me getting the car. I wanted to go ahead and get it over with and take the consequences. I told him I didn't have any trouble borrowing the money at the bank and nobody had to co-sign my note for me. I told him that Mr. Pounds drove it home and it was sitting out behind the barn. I said, "Please don't whip me for getting it; I feel like the Lord just opened up doors for me because it was no problem getting it." I told Harry, "I won't drive it unless I get permission from you, please let me keep it." He sat down at the kitchen table, started to laugh and said, "I don't believe it." I sat down in a chair at the table with him and said, "Honey, that is the God's truth, I am going to pay $45 a month and I know I can do that." He was still in shock, but thank God he was laughing instead of cussing.

He asked for the keys to the car, got up and went out to the barn where the car was. He was outside for about thirty minutes and then he drove the car up into the yard. I was watching him out the window, he had the hood raised, looked at the motor, and then he hollered, "Kathy, come out here." I went out there not knowing what to expect and Harry pulled the oil stick out and said, "The oil is a little low; I am going to show you how to keep it checked, cause it will use a little oil along." By this time my heart was jumping with joy, because I knew he approved of me having the car. I say, "Thank you Jesus," underneath my breath. He said, "You have really surprised me but it looks like a pretty good old

Good Old Yellow Maverick

car. I reckon you can keep it, but you better follow the rules." I said, "Yes sir, you won't have any problem out of me. I won't drive it anywhere until I ask you first." I knew God wasn't going to let me down, I believed it was meant for me to have the car.

After that I practiced driving a little bit everyday for a month in the pasture behind the barn. I got to driving pretty good and I decided it was time to get my driver's license. My girlfriend, Doris, took me to the driver's license testing station. It was slightly raining that day. I passed my written test without any problem, but I was a little nervous when I took the road test. The officer giving me the driving portion of the test had felt a little sorry for me. It was wet and rainy, and I drove the car off of the highway down in a low area with a mud puddle. I scared him a little, but I finally got back up on the road and I said to him, "I am a little nervous, please pass my driving so I can get my license, because I have just bought a car." We went back to the driving station and the driving examiner passed my driving test. He told me to be careful and take it slow. I was so excited, I gave him a big hug and said, "God bless you."

One Sunday, I decided I wanted to try to drive to church. Of course, I got permission from Harry first. It was the first time I had been out on the road, so I prayed, "Lord protect me and put angels all the way around this car. Put an angel here in the driving seat with me and don't let me have a wreck." I didn't have help at all in learning to drive except from God. When I drove to church that first day, I was a little nervous as I was preparing to get ready to go. It was cold weather and I had put a quilt over my son, Jeff, since the heater on the car wouldn't work. Jeff, who was five years old now, joined hands and prayed with me for a safe trip. He was so excited because we never got to go anywhere much and he said, "Mama, don't be afraid, we have a way to go now." I had driven down the road about two or three miles and then all of the sudden, I started singing praises to the Lord, "Jesus loves me, Jesus loves me, this

I know, for the Bible tells me so." A strength came over me from heaven. The fear of driving left me instantly. I started driving that car, and I drove everyday and wasn't scared anymore. I kept on my side of the road. I never got in a hurry while driving. It was like the Lord had just given me the knowledge and sense to drive this old Maverick. I prayed over this old car so much, that I honest to goodness believed that this old car was anointed by God. Now, I had a way to go to church, to work, to Jeff's school for the PTA meetings and to the grocery store. I never went anywhere but those four places. I never did drive unless I asked Harry because I knew he would get mad and take the car away from me if I didn't get permission. He was amazed that I had gotten the car, and that I could drive as well as I could. This was my first car, and I felt so independent and blessed.

12
Where's Harry?

One day when I came home from work, I changed clothes and put on a loose jump suit over my nylon hose. Of course, I always enjoyed running around the house barefoot. I put a large pot roast on top of the stove to cook and put a lid on the big pot. I guess it had been cooking for ten minutes or so when the water started to boil out of the pot onto the stove. I went over and took the pot off the stove; I slipped and fell down on the floor. The scalding hot water and roast spilled in my lap and down my legs. I screamed from the immediate pain of the boiling water as it was frying my legs. The grease that was in the water did not make it any less painful. I felt like I was on fire as I began to feel my skin peel off. I tried to get the clothes off of me, but it pulled the skin more.

Jeff walked in about the time this happened; I hollered, "Run to the neighbors and get help!" My husband was not at home as usual. I had managed to get the jump suit and panty hose off of me, but I was in severe pain by this time. Within minutes Mrs. Modean came over and took me to the local hospital where they admitted me. It was my second time to stay in a hospital overnight. I laid in the bed with the sheet supported up off my lower body because I couldn't stand for anything to touch me. I had second and third degree burns, and then a bad infection set up in my body. I ran a high fever and the burns made my joints stiff. I had to have lots of physical therapy because my whole body had just drawn up from being burned. I was about twenty-four years old when this happened. Several people from the church and the factory came and visited me. I didn't realize I had as many friends as I did because I got several get well cards and even flowers from them. My boss, Mrs. Fairy

Mae Cox, from the pants factory even came by to see me and prayed for me. That made me feel so special coming from her.

I stayed in the hospital for thirty-seven days because I was burned so severely. The hospital I was in was about ten miles from home and Harry never bothered to come see me. It wasn't long distance either to phone, and Harry didn't even take the time to call. But, ironically he must have told some of his customers on his produce route about me getting burned and being in the hospital because some of them sent me cards and flowers. Harry was just peculiar and hard to figure out.

Diane, my sister, had come to the hospital to get me the day I was discharged. She took me home; Jeff my son was still in school and Harry was still at work. When my husband came home that day from work, I asked him, "Honey, why couldn't you have at least just called me eventhough you didn't come to see me?" I just wanted to know why. I didn't fuss; I just asked the question. He had a cussing fit! He said, "There wasn't a d_ _ _ thing that I could have done for you; can't you see that I am working day and night?"

There was a flowerpot sitting on the kitchen cabinet; he picked it up and threw it at me. It hit me in the back of my left leg and I went down on the floor. He came over and stomped me with his big foot repeatedly. I was screaming and crying because I had just gotten out of the hospital from severe leg burns and was being beaten on my bandaged legs. After he beat me, he walked out of the house. I just lay there in the floor for a while because I was in so much pain. I thought, "I am in the jaws of death again with this cruel monster that I am married to." He stayed outside for about an hour or two then he came in and acted like nothing had happened. By this time I had managed to get into the bed. I cried and cried, but I was too scared to do anything. I didn't know what to do. It was really a relief, being in the hospital so long and being away from him. I felt hopeless; all I could do was pray. I was home about a month before I was strong enough to go back to work. I healed fast because I wanted to hurry up and get out of the house.

Harry finally let me keep all of my paycheck. He worked and had his own money. I worked and had my own money. We didn't own anything together and we didn't have anything together. He never did anything for me, not even as much as changing the oil in my car. We would split the bills. Harry would pay the light bill, and I would pay the gas bill. He would pay the rent, and I'd buy the groceries. I'd take care of my car and my personal things. I was very conservative with my money.

Now I wanted a change in my job, I was tired of sewing and wanted to make more money. I got another job at the Macon hospital in the housekeeping department making $6.00 an hour. I worked at the hospital from one in the afternoon until ten o'clock at night. I washed windows, vacuumed the hall carpets, watered the plants and cleaned the doctor's offices after everyone had left everyday. It was a good job because I could hang loose and work without being under pressure. I had enjoyed the time being alone in my own little world. At least while I was at work I was safe, and I did not have to deal with any problems. I kept my distance from the other workers. I was having family problems and didn't want anyone to know. I tried to hold my head up and act like I was fine.

There was one of the housekeepers, a black lady named Beverly, that worked in another part of the hospital and gradually got acquainted with me. She had a quiet loving spirit about her, and I could tell she was a strong Christian lady. She was very friendly toward me and she got to talking about her personal life. She acted like she needed a friend as well as I did. For some reason I gradually got close to her. She said to me one day whenever we were at the mop closet, "Lets get in here and pray." We got in that tiny mop closet, joined hands and cried out to the Lord to help us in our marriages. We were both just so broken hearted.

From that day forward it seemed like a thousand pounds was lifted off of me because I believed God had sent me a true friend. We became prayer partners and buddies in everything we did. I knew I could confide in her and she could confide in me and it would be kept a secret. We are best friends to this day.

Jeff would go to his grandmothers and stay most of the time. My mother-in-law, Mrs. Sawyer was so good about helping take care of Jeff. He always loved to go to his grandmother's, because she would spoil him. By Jeff staying with her, she saved me baby-sitting money. I began to put my money in savings and prayed that one day I would have enough money to leave, once my son was older. I still took the beatings whenever they'd come. Harry would come and go with his fits. I just had to buy some time and wait for my son to be grown up. So I worked and stayed away from home as much as I could. Jeff would stay with his grandparents a lot so I didn't have to worry about him. I felt that working was my only survival to stay sane. As long as I was at work, I didn't have to worry about Harry raving at me.

13
Good Bye Daddy

It had been almost fifteen years since I last laid eyes on Mr. Floyd Edwards, my birth father. He told me when I was a little girl that I was his daughter; I always kept that in my heart, believing that he really was. I thought of him very often and I prayed daily that I would see him again some day. My heart had ached just to know where he was. I felt so broken hearted, so robbed of not having a connection with him. Every daughter wants to be a part of her daddy's life.

It was a cool windy March day and I had been thinking about my daddy an awful lot that day. I had just come into the house from working at the hospital and the phone was ringing. It was my sister calling and telling me mama was in the hospital in another town with pneumonia. My sister told me that Mama was pretty sick and I should go see her. I told her, "Thanks for calling, I will go visit her a little later." Harry came in the house and I asked him if I could drive my car and go stay with Mama at the hospital, "she is very sick and I feel like I should stay with her tonight." Harry gave me permission to go. When I got to the hospital receptionist desk, I looked to see which room Mama was in. I got a big shock as I was reading the list of names that were in the hospital. There in black and white was the name I had been praying for; Floyd Edwards, room 220, two rooms down from mama's room. "Oh, my God, thank you, thank you."

I thought I was about to have a heart attack because I was shaking so badly. I could hardly believe it. I walked down the long hall to the door of daddy's room. I took a deep breath and tried to pull myself together before I walked in. I was thinking, I don't know what to say or what to do. It was going through my mind, I hope he still remembers me, because it had been so long. I pushed the door open slowly and looked in the hospital bed; I walked to the foot of the bed and I said quivering, "I am Kathy Telson and I just wanted to check and see how Mr. Edwards is doing." There was a lady sitting in the corner of the room that got up out of her chair and walked to me and said tearfully, "It is you." I think, "Does she know, who is she, or what." She said, "Your daddy had told me all about you; Floyd is dying and his last request was he wished he could see you before he leaves this world."

I started to cry and I felt helpless; I pulled away from her and I walked up beside daddy's bed. I put my hand on his hand; I got down in his face with tears rolling down my cheeks and I said, "Daddy, it's me, Kathy, I'm here, I love you and I have missed you so much all these years." He looked at me with tears in his eyes and with a whisper and said, "I love you too." I could see daddy was very weak and he was really unable to talk much. I told him, "I am here to stay with you all night, don't try to talk because I know it hurts you." I told Daddy, "Squeeze my hand if you can understand me." He had his eyes open, looked at me with a little bit of a grin and barely squeezed my hand because he was so sick. I sat down on his bed; I rubbed daddy's face very gently and just looked at him and cried silently. I was in as much pain as he was but I was so thankful to be here with him even though I knew our time together was very short. His wife told me she was going to go outside for a while and give us some time alone.

I wanted to say so much to Daddy, but I knew that it was too late. He moved the respirator away from his mouth and started coughing real hard. I tried to pat him on the back as he was trying to get his breath; daddy finally got straightened out and motioned for me to raise his head up. I put a pillow under his head so he could sit up some in the bed. He tried to talk, telling me he was so sorry for everything. I told him it was okay; I am here with you now.

I felt like I needed to ask him if he had the Lord in his life. I wanted daddy to go to heaven because I knew he was dying. Still crying, I asked him if he wanted to ask Jesus to forgive him of his sins. With tears in his eyes, he told me, "Yes, pray for me." I led him in a sinner's prayer; Daddy asked Jesus to come into his heart and forgive him of all his sins. He squeezed my hand tight, looked up at me again and told me, "I am so sorry, please believe me." I told Daddy, "I understand, try to get some rest because you are so weak, I am right here by your side."

As he was dozing off, his wife walked back in, she talked to me and said, "Floyd has lived with the guilt for years because he hasn't been a part of your life." She told me that my daddy couldn't help the circumstances. Mama and he had made lots of mistakes, and I was the one that had paid the price. Mrs. Edwards said, "I know you are hurt and I am so sorry." I told her that it didn't matter; that it was all over now. The rest of the night was just silence in the dark; I didn't want to ask her any questions, because it did not matter. Maybe I just didn't want to know more; I was finally having some closure.

It was about daylight and I knew it was time to go home. Mrs. Edwards and I were standing there by his bed. I looked at my daddy with my heart ripped to pieces; I touched him for the last time and said, "I love you." I kissed him on the forehead as he was trying to mumble, "I love you too." I had to pull myself away from him as I walked out of the room so broken hearted. Mrs. Edwards walked out with me and we hugged each other, all I could say was, "I am so sorry." I sadly walked away.

I never went to see Mama while she was in the hospital; I was actually sicker than mama was from all the heartache she had helped cause me. As I drove home I knew that was the last time I would see my daddy and I thanked the Lord for answering my prayers, "He wasn't a day late." I was home about twenty minutes and the phone rang. Mrs. Edwards was on the phone and she said, "Kathy, your daddy died five minutes after you left. I told her, "I know; thank you for calling." I felt like I had my time with my daddy that night I stayed at the hospital beside his bed, and that was my funeral. I could not take anymore pain or heartache. From that day forward I have kept the memory of my daddy inside of me and have never talked about him anymore. The pain is too deep!

14
On The Run

It was a beautiful Saturday morning in the month of May. I was feeling depression setting in heavy on me and was very tired in body as I was trying to prepare breakfast that morning. I felt low as a dog and had a sick feeling that I was a "pure old no good for nothing." I was feeling everything Harry had dished out to me in my spirit and I was grieving silently over my daddy. Harry had already beaten my mind into the ground so much until I was a walking time bomb ready to explode. His words were so cruel and I was still thinking I was a nobody. It didn't make any difference how much I tried to bathe myself, I could not feel clean or good about myself. I thought I was going to wash my skin raw. The feeling inside me from all the abuse made me feel empty, numb, ashamed, degraded and embarrassed. I couldn't feel like a normal person was supposed to feel. I was a cold empty shell. At night when I had to lie down with Harry I would grit my teeth, shut my eyes and pray for the agony to hurry up and go away. Every bone in my body would ache and tighten up; I hated for him to touch me. I would plead with him not to do it; he would slap me across the face and go ahead anyway. I prayed to die daily because of all the pain I was carrying inside of me.

I told God I was losing my mind, my hurt was down deep in the root of my soul. I thought I was the cause of it all, I wasn't pretty or good enough at all to make Harry love me, and that was why he treated me so badly. He constantly reminded me, I was the kid he bought off Telson Hill and I wasn't worth the salt that went in my bread. I lived with the feeling of a very low self-esteem. So finally the next day on Sunday I took my chances to leave. I went to church as usual; there was a couple in the church, Ricky and Lona Cross who traveled different places across the states on business trips. One of their business stops was at the PTL Club in North Carolina. My son and I left with them that Sunday afternoon. Ricky and Lona were good Christian people and tried to help me escape from the bad situation I was in. They supplied me with money and clothing and had connections to get me a job at PTL until I could get on my feet.

The PTL was a Christian ministry with a village of restaurants, hotels, churches, a prayer chapel, parks for the children to play in and all kinds of shops and businesses. There was plenty of work for people to help in the ministry and a Christian school for the children to attend. There were plenty of activities to keep the children occupied and adequate security so that I didn't have to worry about protection for Jeff or myself.

My son and I rented a little twenty foot camper trailer for fifty dollars a week to live in there on the camp grounds of the PTL village. Our trailer had a small refrigerator, a gas cook stove with two burners and a little oven. The table was in a little cubical that converted into a bed. The bathroom had a tiny sink, a mini toilet and a small shower. It was big enough for Jeff and me, and we were as happy living in it as if it was the finest mansion on a hill. Every night before we went to bed, we would get down on our knees beside our small bed and ask God to put angels all the way around our little home. This was the first place that I actually felt like was my own home, where I could be myself and feel safe. There were several other trailers in the village, a big lake near by with picnic tables; it was just a good environment for everyone that lived or visited there.

I got a job at the Little Horse Restaurant as a hostess and enjoyed welcoming people and then taking them to their tables. The job was so easy that I would have worked for nothing. I stayed busy trying not to think about where I came from, and I did not want anyone to know about my past. I worked in the daytime and at night Jeff and I went to church. I needed all the spiritual help I could get. I had everything right here that I needed, a good job, a warm safe home, my son, my car, a little money, a loving church and peace of mind. Life seemed too good to be true right now for me. This was the happiest I had ever been in my whole life. My nerves were starting to settle down, and I was beginning to sleep at night. I knew there were guards on duty around the clock and that made me feel even more safe.

When I had spare time, Jeff and I would walk around the village park. We visited the shops and the ice cream parlor and Jeff always liked the train ride that went around the lake. There was always some kind of entertainment going on, gospel singing, puppet shows and organized ball games for the children.

Things were going good and I was glad to be hid out from Harry. I didn't tell family or friends where I was; I couldn't take any chances of Harry finding us. We had been there for about two weeks and had gotten settled in good. We had made friends and I really did love the new environment I was in.

Then early one morning about daybreak the guard that watched over the entrance of the PTL village came to my little trailer. He knocked on my door and woke me up. I opened the door and he said, "There is some man looking for you." My heart fell at my feet and I started shaking all over. The guard said, "Calm down, it's not all that bad." I thought, "He has no idea of what is fixin' to happen." The guard continued to tell me, "There is a man here from out of state with a picture of you and your son. He says he is your husband." I thought, "I can't believe this, I am not safe any more, he has found out where I am." The guard told me that Harry said he had found Jesus in his heart and was looking for his family so he can put it back together again and that he needed to find me because he loved me very much. The last time that Harry had told me he loved me was on the day we got married. I thought, "what a crock of bull he is telling." I knew it was a trap to get to me. I was grown up now and I knew better than to trust or believe him, I knew Harry's lies. About that time Harry drove up to the trailer and ran to my door carrying on like he was madly in love with me. Harry said, "I have missed y'all so much and I have just about grieved myself to death over you. I have looked and called everywhere I could think of trying to find you." Harry told me all kinds of stuff to try to make me feel good.

Harry said, "I went to the mailbox and there was a card for Jeff. It was a welcome back card from PTL telling him to come back and visit his Sunday school class in North Carolina. I then knew where you were and have driven all night to get here."

Jeff was just a child and he didn't know any better than to give the church our old address. I had always taught Jeff to remember our address in case of emergency and I had not taught him our new address here in North Carolina. That was a card sent out mistakenly and fell right in Harry's hands.

Harry tried to convince us he was sorry for his mistakes and that he wanted us back. Harry was shedding some tears for the first time that I could ever remember. He said, "I went to church this past Sunday, and I realized I have been a mean man. Kathy, I am sorry and I want to make it up to you. I want you to come back home and give me another chance." I didn't want him and I didn't want to go back. Even though Harry was a little emotional I didn't trust him; I knew he was a devil in sheep's clothing.

Harry stayed a couple days trying to convince me to go back home. He tried first the nice way and after he saw I wasn't going home, he then threatened me. Harry packed Jeff's things and put him in the car and said, "We are going home with or without you." I wasn't going to be without my son. Harry knew Jeff was my life and that he had me where he wanted me. I was scared and felt like I didn't have a choice. I didn't want to get anybody involved from the village and the Cross family had already left to go back home.

Again I realized how Harry controlled me like I was a piece of his

PTL-Little Horse Restaurant, Where I Worked

property and I was still reminded of how he bought me off Telson Hill "for a hundred pound sack of potatoes." I will carry those words with me for as long as I live. How could I ever forget when he continuously mentioned it? So here I was again, going back to the devils den. I had no trust at all in him or that he was a changed man. First of all he will have to prove himself to me.

I came back home and Harry lets me find another job. I went to work at a local plant making $9.00 an hour working on the production line. I was very grateful having a job making this much money and the work was fairly easy. I was glad to work because it kept me away from Harry. Home life was better than it was, but not all that great. I just worked and tried not to think about it. Again I was going through the motions of life and trying to survive, I kept my mouth shut, and my feelings to myself because I was a prisoner of war. Harry ruled me and I took it because there was no way out and nobody to stand up to him. He made me think he was king. I did exactly what he said; I had no life, no say so about anything, no feelings and I walked this lonely road alone with the Lord. Believe me, it was a hard rough road to walk and I could not have walked it without the Lord. He gave me strength, days that I thought I couldn't go on, He picked me up and carried me.

Time had passed, and my son was sixteen years old. Jeff had so much hurt and pain in him from seeing so much abuse all those years. I helped get him a car to drive and a part time job working after school and in the summer for a man down the road named Eddie who had a house moving business. Eddie felt sorry for Jeff and took him under his wing. Jeff was small and he could crawl under the houses to the tight places where the other workers couldn't get to. Eddie had taught Jeff to do electric and carpenter work. Jeff admired Eddie because Eddie gave him attention and a chance in life. Eddie had two sons close to Jeff's age and took Jeff in just like family. They even took Jeff on vacation to

Florida. Eddie's family was a positive influence on Jeff's life, and I am very grateful that they took an interest in my son.

There had been over sixteen years of abuse now, I had been beaten and stomped on until I didn't know how much more I could take. My body was tired and worn out, I was having health problems with my bones and joints. I was tired of running, hiding, sleepless nights, and not knowing what the next day most likely would bring. I knew if I died I would be in a better place. I was at the point in my life that I was ready for Harry to put a bullet in my head and get it over with. I had my mind made up; the next beating would be his last so he had better make it good. I was at the point I was totally losing it.

I can still remember April 30, the day before I left, like it was yesterday. I'd gotten up like I always did and cooked our Sunday lunch. I put it on the stove so that we'd have it to eat whenever we got back from church. Jeff and I went to church as usual. We had a good service; the sermon was on the family pulling together. Too bad Harry didn't hear this one! After church that Sunday, I came home and put Sunday dinner on the table. After we ate, I was cleaning the dishes and noticed the red priscilla curtains above the big picture window over the sink looked mighty dusty. I took them down and put them in the washer to wash. Harry came in as I was putting up other curtains while the dirty ones were being washed. I was standing on top of the kitchen cabinet, and he came in fussing at me. Harry said hatefully, "I don't like them! I don't like them!" I got off the counter and I said, "Harry, there is no sense in you ranting and raving like that. What is wrong with you? I am just washing the other curtains to get the dust off. I'm going to get them back up when they are washed and done." When I said that, Harry threw my head against the cabinet and started hitting me. He told me that I couldn't talk back to him and said, "You put those SOB's back up, and I mean, put them back up now!" He just kept on hitting me with his fist.

In a rage, he then turned the kitchen table upside down. The salt and pepper shakers along with the sugar bowl smashed on the floor. Then he turned to me, threw me down, shoved my face in the shattered glass on the floor, and kicked me on the backend. Then Harry yelled, "You SOB!" (That was my name whenever he was mad, except he did not abbreviate it.) Harry just kept kicking and screaming at me telling me to clean it up. I was crying and begging him to stop.

Our son walked in the middle of this and started yelling at his daddy to stop. Harry then grabbed Jeff by the hair and dragged him to the back of the house to Jeff's room. He beat him pretty good and told him that if he ever ran off with me again that he would bury us both. He locked Jeff up in his room. Harry came back into the kitchen where I was crying and cleaning up the mess. He walks by and stormed out of the door, slamming it behind him.

Finally, I got it all cleaned up and went back to check on Jeff. He was crying and shaking and said, "Mama, why don't you leave him? He's going to kill you and me both! Please leave! I hate to see you keep going through this." I just grabbed Jeff, held him, and cried so hard with him. We both were all to pieces. He was just sixteen years old. I told him, "I don't want to leave because I don't want to leave you behind, but for now we just have to hold on." We clung to each other. The afternoon passed, Harry stayed outside, and I was glad of it. It was getting close to church time. Jeff and I always went to church on Sunday nights. I was afraid to get the car and go without asking, so I went outside, like a child, and asked my boss, "May I go to church tonight in the car?" Harry looked at me as if nothing had ever happened and said, "Sure, I don't have a problem with that." He went back to working in the barn. I went back in the house, got my Bible and told Jeff we had permission to go to church.

We walked into church hoping that no one would notice my heart was so broken that night. The preacher spoke on love in the home. I felt like that message was directed at me because I had never experienced any love at home, as an adult or as a child. The preacher said that God gave us the strength and the ability to take a stand. He said there are women out there being abused, and God does not desire that; that is not God's will. He said that when it seems like there's no way, that there will be a way if you step out on faith. I was starting to cry and I could feel the Spirit of the Lord. It was so powerful that I felt in my spirit that God had my number. At the end of the service Jeff and I went to the altar and prayed; I cried out so hard to God, asking Him to give me direction and enough supernatural strength and courage to make a final decision. The altar was full that night because there were other hurting women.

That night, I went home and Harry was watching television. I put my Bible up and told Jeff to go to his room. I went into the kitchen and stood at the sink where the incident had happened that day. Harry walked up behind me and began fondling me. I started crying and pleading, "Please, don't touch me. Please don't bother me. You've hurt me enough, just please don't." I broke into tears again; he turned me around and hit me several times in the face. He stood over me again and said, "You are my wife and I'll ____ you anytime I want to." He then took me to the bedroom. When he was through, I got up and started vomiting from the bedroom all the way to the bathroom. My nerves were shot. He went to sleep, and when he did I went to the living room.

I opened up my Bible and the Lord led me to these verses.

Fret not thyself because of evil-doers, neither be thou envious against the workers of iniquity.

For they shall soon be cut down like the grass, and wither as the green herb.

Trust in the Lord, and do good; so shalt thou dwell in the land, and verily thou shalt be fed.

Delight thyself also in the Lord; and he shall give thee the desires of thine heart.

Commit thy way unto the Lord; trust also in him; and he shall bring it to pass.

And he shall bring forth thy righteousness as the light, and thy judgment as the noonday.

Rest in the Lord, and wait patiently for him: fret not thyself because of him who prospereth in his way, because of the man who bringeth wicked devices to pass.

Cease from anger, and forsake wrath: fret not thyself in any wise to do evil.

For evildoers shall be cut off: but those that wait upon the Lord, they shall inherit the earth.

(Psalms 37: 1-9)

    I felt like the Lord was telling me to wait on Him and to trust Him so that He could take care of me. I would receive blessings from God.
    When Harry awoke in a couple hours and found I wasn't in the bed, he came into the living room; grabbed me by the hair and forced me to

come back to the bedroom to sleep with him. I lay awake all night long and prayed. I had saved up enough money by this time to leave. I just thought to myself, "If I live until day break, I'm leaving." My mind was made up and a strength was coming over me that I can't describe. I knew I had to leave, because when I started thinking about the things Harry had done to me I began to have thoughts of revenge. I was afraid I was going to snap and kill him. I had never been totally to this point before.

So, the next morning I got up and did the usual thing. I made coffee and breakfast and laid Harry's clothes out for work. I said to myself, "This will be the last cup of coffee I'll ever fix for him." Then I got him up to go to work. He got up as usual, cussing and hollering. It would take him about an hour to get out of the bed; he was hard to get up.

He finally came in the kitchen and I fixed his coffee while he sat at the kitchen table. I put the coffee in front of him like I did every morning; he took the cup and threw it across the room like a wild demon. He said, "You cripple, ugly SOB." He took me by the hair, shoved my face in a mirror and screamed, "I can fix my own d _ _ _ cup of coffee!" So, I went into the other room and Harry poured his own cup of coffee. This fit was my confirmation letting me know today was the day. Harry drank his coffee, ate his toast, and finally got dressed to go to work. About fifteen or twenty minutes later I was making the bed and he walked in, kissed me and said, "Bye honey, have a good day." It was amazing! He acted like nothing had ever happened. After he left, I broke down and cried for what felt like forever.

15
Finally, Enough Courage

I got Jeff up and told him that I had made up my mind; I was leaving for good and I wanted him to go with me. He said, "Mama, you go and get a divorce first; I am scared to leave with you. You will have to fight daddy in court for me, but I will tell the judge I want to be with you and how mean daddy is to both of us. I can go stay with grandmother; I'm not a kid any more, I'm big enough to take care of myself. I have my car and my job; I will be all right. Please go on without me. I am worried daddy is going to wind up killing you. I knew Jeff was afraid to be without me, but he wanted me to do what I had to do.

I gave him some money and got him off to school. I told him I'd send him some money each week, but I'd have to send it from a different address because I didn't want Harry to know where I was staying. Jeff would be safe with his grandparents, but I hated leaving him. It was the hardest thing I've ever done, but I knew I had to do it. I just had to trust the Lord and put Jeff in God's hands and know he was going to be okay for a little while away from me. My son had always been my life; I hoped and prayed that he really did understand why I was leaving him behind.

So, when Jeff left for school, I left too. I didn't take any clothes except for what I had on my back or anything else with me because I wanted nothing to remind me of my past. I didn't worry about clothes, because I could find plenty at yard sales. I knew that I could make it; I had money saved up, but my main concern was protection.

I went to work that day at the plant; went into the main office and told them that I was having marriage problems. I explained to them the extent of Harry's abuse and I was very ashamed having to tell them. I asked for a leave of absence for about a month. I knew I couldn't be coming to work because Harry would catch me on the way. My supervisor, Mr. Scruggs, told me I was a good employee. I had all my sick days built up from over the years. I never missed work and had even worked days when I was sick. Mr. Scruggs told me that I could have the leave of absence and get paid for it if I had a doctor's statement and that my checks would still come in each week. My nerves were so shot that I actually was sick. I went to the doctor, got the statement, took it back to work and immediately left for the lawyer's office.

I told the lawyer about the years of abuse and that my husband was a crazy man; that I did not want anything and didn't want to deal with him over a custody battle for Jeff. I just wanted a divorce with joint custody of our son. I wanted no child support, no money, nothing; I just wanted out, permanently! My lawyer didn't like it, but I told him to do it my way or I'd find someone else to do it for me. The lawyer said, "If Jeff is sixteen years old, he can decide for himself where he wants to go. You need to sign an order of protection that is called a restraining order. We will file the papers and Mr. Sawyer will get them in a few days."

I had no family I could depend on to protect me and didn't want to get anybody else involved. I drove to another town where I knew Harry did not ever go. I got a motel room close by a hospital and parked my car in the hospital parking lot, I was afraid to leave my car parked at the motel. I had to think safe. I was so afraid of Harry finding me. I didn't tell a soul where I was. I had to do this on my own, and I couldn't afford to trust anybody.

After three or four days had passed, I decided that I had to do something. I couldn't just sit here and deplete my money in this motel room. It cost too much. I got to thinking about the little trailer I lived in while I was in North Carolina. I thought, "I am going to go looking for me a little trailer to live in." I got in my car and rode around in some trailer parks. I didn't find anything available there. However, about ten miles down the road from the motel where I was staying, I noticed a twenty-five foot camping trailer sitting on the side of the road in a yard. I drove up and looked at it; it seemed like it was in good shape. I walked up to the people's house and asked about it. It had a stove, sink, bathroom and a half bed. I thought that this was all I needed. I bought it for $500.00. It just so happened the man that I bought the trailer from owned the trailer park where I had been earlier. He got it moved into his trailer park and charged me $75 a month to park it there. I was amazed at how everything fell right into place. I knew God was smiling on me. I got the lights and water turned on and thought to myself, "I have a roof over my head; I can make it now."

I went to the supermarket, got me some snacks to eat on and then went to the dollar store. I wasn't thinking about food, I was just thinking about staying hid out. I bought some bed sheets, a blanket, a couple of towels, washcloths, and some toilet paper. I just bought the necessary things; this was all I needed to get by on. I had to be careful spending my money. This little trailer would do me for now because I never knew if I would have to leave the town or even the country. I managed okay except I was missing Jeff really bad.

Thirty days later when it came time to go to court for the divorce, I was very shaky. Harry had never gotten his divorce papers because he wouldn't go to the door when the police officers tried to serve them. My attorney had the papers mailed to mine and Harry's house. I got a girlfriend to check the mailbox when I knew Harry was at work. She checked the mailbox that whole week to see if the divorce papers had come. When his divorce papers came, she got them out of the mailbox, because we didn't want Harry to know the day I would appear in court. The mailbox was legally as much mine as it was his, so I didn't break any law. I had to cover my tracks. I knew there would be trouble before hand if Harry found out he was being divorced, besides he thought I didn't have sense enough or the courage to file for a divorce anyway.

Finally, the day came. I was real nervous and I kept looking around the courtroom. I didn't see any sign of Harry and this gave me some relief. The court session began and mine was the first case to come up. When the judge granted me an absolute divorce, I just wept, I hated it had to come to this, but I didn't have any choice. I wished my marriage could have worked out because deep down I really did love him. That is why I stayed for sixteen and a half years, hoping and praying Harry would change and treat me like he really loved me. Divorce is never easy; no one wins.

I walked out of the courtroom that day a free woman. I had the money I had been saving and now for the first time in my life I was totally free. The next day I called Harry and said, "We need to talk, meet me tomorrow at one o'clock at the Bonanza Steak House," and hung up. I met him the next day in the restaurant parking lot. I had two policemen sitting in their police cars in plain view in the parking lot. Harry thought we were going to have a lovely dinner, sit, and talk. What a surprise Harry was about to get! Harry drove up and parked beside my car. I got out and stood at the back of my car with my divorce papers in my hand. Harry got out of his car and walked back to where I was and tried to embrace me saying, "I have looked everywhere in the world for you." I pushed him away and handed him the divorce papers saying, "Here, I need to give you these divorce papers; you are a free man now." He grabbed me and when he did the cops got out of their car, came over and held him while I got away. I left and went back to my trailer. I had a restraining order against him but I knew that if he found me the law would be meaningless. I stayed confined to my trailer mostly and hoped Harry wouldn't find me.

A month had passed and I went back to work. I lived in my trailer for six months and Harry never found out where I lived. I was beginning to feel cramped in such small living quarters. So I found myself a house and bought it. This was my first house as a free woman. It was a two bed room white frame house. I built a white plank fence across the front yard. My place was like a little dollhouse.

In the beginning Jeff would stay with his daddy part time and with me part time. A couple of months passed and Harry decided to let Jeff move in with me permanently. He thought that if Jeff stayed with me I wouldn't have the opportunity to meet anyone else. That was Harry's main concern. But that was my least concern.

16
Rough Days

Harry let me rest for a few days, and then he started harassing me again. Harry would call and cry and beg me to give him another chance. I remember nights that Harry would lay in a ditch outside my house and wait for me to get home. I always kept the weeds trimmed down so it wasn't so easy for him to hide. I tried to think of everything because I knew that he would be out there sooner or later. Sure enough, Harry was and he tried to break into my house. It was still a war even though I was divorced. Friends told me I should have shot him, but I was not that kind of person.

One night I came in from work and I looked out in the yard to see if anything looked suspicious. Sometimes I'd call the police to escort me into my house because I was so afraid. Anyway, the police came that night and looked around. They didn't see anyone. I thought that he was home that night and I would get to have a good night's rest. It was about one in the morning when I laid down. I was dead tired and went to sleep quickly. About two o'clock in the morning I woke up with Harry standing over me. I screamed, Harry grabbed my arms and started telling me how much he loved me. He said that he wouldn't ever hurt me again. The whole time I was fighting and kicking at him. He then hit me and raped me. He told me he was going to kill me. He had a 22-caliber pistol and pointed it at me; I was begging him not to kill me. Harry would stop at nothing, he said that he was going to kill me and then himself too. Harry had cut the phone lines and climbed upstairs in the attic and was waiting until I came home and had gone to sleep. Harry had gotten a key to my house out of Jeff's pocket while Jeff was spending the weekend with him. That was how he was able to get in and attack me that night.

It was daylight now on Saturday morning. Jeff didn't come in that night because he stayed at a friend's house. The lights were on in the living room. My brother, Donnie, lived right down the road and he would leave at about 4:45 in the morning to go to work. He passed by my house and saw the lights were on; became concerned and pulled up in the driveway. When he did that, Harry ran out the back door. I ran to the front door and told Donnie to call the police because my phone lines were cut. I then told him what had happened.

When the police finally got there, Harry was long gone. I told them the deal about Harry. The police officers wanted me to sign a warrant and I knew that if I signed that warrant, he would be out of jail in no time because he had money. I knew it would aggravate Harry and just make him more dangerous, so I wouldn't sign the warrant. I had called the police several times before and since I lived in the county it took them about thirty minutes to get to my house. I told the police then that I wasn't going to call them anymore and I didn't. They said that the restraining order would keep him away but it didn't do me any good. Harry got away every time. This kind of behavior went on for about a year after my divorce. It was almost like being married again. I was still scared and had no protection. This war was a nightmare from the depths of hell.

My health was getting worse and I felt tired all the time; but how could I get any rest with all the baggage hanging on me. I would get up in the morning and be stiff in my joints, I could barely move from the stiffness in my feet and legs; my hands would draw in a stiff position where I couldn't bend my fingers. The fluid I retained in my body made me swell up so big that I would look like a fattening hog. Some days I couldn't even dress myself. I finally got so bad that I called my son to come and take me to the hospital. I was so drawn in my body that he had to dress me; Jeff picked me up and carried me to his car. We went to the emergency room and he got one of the nurses to help get me out of the car. They examined and admitted me into the hospital. The doctor ran tests to see what was causing my problem. My feet were burning like fire, my swollen fingers felt like they had needles sticking in them and my back was cutting me into. I was in severe pain and after several days I was diagnosed with lupus and rheumatoid arthritis. These are diseases that affect the immune system, your joints, bones and blood cells.

I was mentally drained and now this has come on me. I never could understand why all this was happening to me. It took a long time to get this disease in control and into remission. This was in 1989 and I am still under a doctor's care today. I have good and bad days; I just have to take it one day at a time. I pray to God daily to give me strength to overcome these trials in life.

My son Jeff began to totally withdraw from me, he was involved with friends that were the wrong crowd. They were experimenting with marijuana. Jeff's girlfriend Angie was seventeen years old and was seven months pregnant with his child. Well, instead of me going to pieces and crying in my pity because of all my problems, I prayed a little harder for God's help. I tried to help fix my son's mistakes and take part of the blame for his choices because I felt guilty for what he went through all his life. The child was bound to turn to something or someone for some relief. Jeff's pain was deep down and was tormenting him every day of his life. Jeff was seventeen years old when he married Angie and started himself a new life.

I took the money I had saved for Jeff to go to college and bought a house trailer and an acre lot for them to set up housekeeping. I fixed the trailer up with all the furnishings necessary for their home. I sewed curtains and helped Angie decorate it up like a little dream house. I knew it wouldn't be but a couple months before the baby would be here. Some of my friends and myself gave Angie a nice baby shower to get some things for the baby. I knew it was going to be rough on them because they were both so young and were having a lot of responsibility put on them.

Jeff quit school three months before graduation day and went to work full time to make a living for his family. I helped them every way that I could and neglected myself. I put all my energy into trying to make their lives more comfortable. I loved Angie and she was the daughter I always wanted. She was a good mother and excellent wife to Jeff. I knew she had her hands full; Jeff was a very troubled young man carrying wounds from the past. He had gotten out of church and had left God totally out of his life.

I hardly ever went back home to Telson Hill and visit. Mama was still hateful to me even though I was grown up now. I stayed away because there is still too much of a mess going on in the family. Rozen divorced Mama after forty-seven years of marriage. He gave her the house and all the land except for a small lot next to mama's house. Rozen bought a house trailer and put it in mama's yard on the lot he kept beside her house. He put up a private fence between Mama's house and his trailer so Mama couldn't see everything that was going on. Rozen continued to party, drink, gamble and bring home wild women.

Rozen slowed down a bit after a year and married a woman that was half his age, Barbara Holback. She loved whiskey and all that went with it. She also loved Rozen's money being handed over to her. Wasn't this a big mess, and in mama's own yard! It was embarrassing for the community to drive by and see what was going on. Fortunately, all of us kids had already left home. Mama looked across the fence and still wanted to be a part of what was going on. Rozen stayed married for a bout six months and his wife left; she had gotten all she wanted out of him. Rozen was now broke; down to nothing except for a little social security check. He had sold all of his livestock and farm equipment and had nothing left to show in return. Rozen had sowed his wild oats until he was nothing but a sick old man now.

Soon afterward Rozen took sick with a stroke and was hospitalized for some time. Well, Mama said he was not going to any nursing home. She got a hospital bed, put it in her home and brought Rozen back to her house. She waited on him hand and foot, bathed and dressed him, did therapy on his joints to get movement back into his body and fed him. Mama nursed Rozen for about nine months and got him back to good health from the stroke. Rozen was like new again, had a new lease on life and was looking for new territory to explore. Mama must have really loved Rozen or else she was as sick as he was. Rozen was up on his feet for about two weeks and then moved next door back into his old ragged trailer.

Rozen got to going with a trashy woman called, "Little Bit," that he met at a beer joint and fell "head over hills" in love with her. She was young enough to be his daughter. Rozen always had a thing for younger women. Little Bit stayed with Rozen for several months, and then she left and lived with one of Rozen's black friends Mr. Pete, a drinking buddy. Mr. Pete had often worked around the farm doing odd jobs for Rozen. He and Rozen swapped up with this trashy girl. Little Bit never stayed over two days at a time with either one of them. The gossip was terrible in the community. One day Little Bit was on Telson Hill with Rozen, and two days later she would be over at Mr. Pete's sitting on the front porch drinking beer and whiskey. All I could say for the whole sick bunch was, "God help them." It was a shame and disgrace to the whole community. For several months this went on, and Mama was still running and begging Rozen to come back home to her. She loved him and it didn't make any difference what he did, she just wanted old Rozen back home. One cold day in January Rozen came home from drinking and fell out of his truck into a big mud hole in the front yard. Rozen is a big man so Mama called two of the boys to come and get him up and into his house. Rozen had his girlfriend, Little Bit, with him and Diane, my sister, just happened to be visiting Mama that day. Diane was so mad about Mama nursing Rozen back to health and now here he was on the hill with another woman. Diane went out in the yard and picked up a tomato stick. She got a hold of Little Bit and beat the crap out of her with the stick. She said, "I'll teach you a lesson to come up here drunk with Rozen after Mama has waited on him day and night." Little Bit takes off running down the road. There never was a dull moment on Telson Hill.

Mama checked on him the next morning and he was really sick; he could hardly move. They carried him to the hospital and admitted him. He went into a coma and lay there for about a week. Mama almost had a heart attack fearing she was about to lose him. She never left Rozen's side.

Little Bit and Mr. Pete heard about Rozen being in the hospital bad off. They came to the hospital; Mr. Pete waited in the hall talking to one of my brothers while Little Bit reluctantly came into Rozen's room. Of course, Mama was sitting there at Rozen's side, holding his hand. Little Bit came in crying her eyes out and asked mama, "Do you mind if I see Rozen, we were so close, but I don't want to cause no trouble?" Mama and all of us girls were there. Luckily for Little Bit, Diane had gone to get something to eat. Mama says, "No, I don't mind, I can't be mean to you, cause you love him just like I do." Little Bit went over to Rozen's bedside and shook him trying to wake him up. She was very emotional and said to Rozen, "Pappy, wake up, Little Bit is here. Get up, let's go to town and have a beer." One of the girls walked over to her and told her, "Rozen is dying, he won't be drinking no more beer. Honey, it's almost over." The nurse called the family in and said, "He's gasping for breath and it won't be very long until he is gone." The nurse said, "He is holding on for you children to say your good byes or to settle anything between you, if there is anything you need to tell him you need to do it now, you don't need any regrets."

The last four younger children that were still at home, after I left home, took it very hard. Don't ask me why, but they cried and carried on like he was a prince. Rozen's funeral was one that people won't forget. They buried Rozen in a red flannel shirt, new overalls which is what he wore all the time and a denim jacket. They put a package of King Edward cigars in the bib of his overalls and pictures of every child and thirty-seven grandchildren in his billfold. Rozen never was totally broke, so they wanted to send money with him on his way. Each child contributed money and a few of the wealthier sons put in hundred dollar bills. I was told that one of his drinking buddies had put a pair of dice, a deck of poker cards and a pint of whiskey in his casket. I didn't check to see if this was so, because I hardly looked at him and I couldn't have cared less.

About two hundred people attended Rozen's funeral. Rozen's drinking and gambling buddies came; people he did horse trading with over the years came; friends of us kids were there and women Rozen had fooled with over the years also came, including "Little Bit." I am sure some came just out of curiosity. You would have thought he was a saint, people were in such despair. I could not shed a tear; I was totally numb. When I glanced at Rozen in the casket I could not feel anything one way or the other; it was sad because the rest of the family was pitiful.

Harry sent a big flower arrangement and came to the funeral. He walked up to me and tried to console me; I pushed him away and said, "I am okay, I don't have a reason to grieve." It was coming back into my mind of how he and Rozen had made deals over me. I was a shattered glass broken into so many pieces. It was all I could do, just to focus on getting by from day to day. I still felt like I was an outsider. I did not belong there; I was only there for my brothers and sisters.

My brothers and sisters bought Rozen a tombstone to go on his grave; it was very unusual. They all paid a hundred dollars each on the rock. For whatever the reason was, one of my brothers, Chuckie, voluntarily paid my part with no questions asked. On the rock was a farm scene with a house, barn, tractor, old truck and all kinds of livestock in the pasture with a fence around the home place. The rock looked like us Telsons lived on a big prosperous farm with all the rich trimmings, not the rat hole we actually lived in. On the backside of the rock was a team of mules pulling an old wagon with a farmer sitting in the driver's seat with the caption, "Look at what followed me home." Underneath was a list of all the children's names listed in big letters. Rozen's funeral and tombstone cost more than the old house I was raised up in. I didn't have any part in Rozen's funeral arrangements or the tombstone either. My say so wouldn't have made any difference anyway. I know we have a merciful God and I hope Rozen had made things right with Him before he died.

With the scars of all those hurtful experiences lodged deep in my heart, I often wondered whether God could ever use me or heal me. I kept my past embedded to myself, for I soon discovered that most people are too preoccupied with their own lives to bear someone else's burdens. I didn't trust people; I feared that if they found out about my past, I would only be rejected again and again.

There were other relationships in my life during the ten years after I left Harry, but these did not involve physical abuse. I was so mentally drained and confused that I could not enjoy a normal life with another man. My past was embedded in me too deep. I was damaged material.

17
Healing

I moved to Memphis to get away from Harry's harassment and to be nearer to my doctor because my health wasn't getting any better. So I moved into an apartment with two other girls, Sheila and Candy, for about 4 months. They were good to me and helped take care of me while I was sick. They knew I was emotionally drained and near my road's end. We had just buried Rozen a few days ago and for some reason a crying spell just came on me and I cried for three days. I can't understand the reason why, since I couldn't cry at his funeral, but all I could do was cry my eyes out. Rozen's death was nothing to cry about, but the old saying is, "It is all over now, but for the crying." My girlfriend, Sheila, realized something was severely wrong and talked me into going to the doctor.

I went to a clinic and asked to talk to Dr. Stan Long. I broke down in his office and said, "I can't deal with life, I need some help. I'm totally losing it." Dr. Long suggested I needed some counseling and made arrangements for me to be admitted into a counseling clinic at Lakeside Hospital. I thought I was losing control with reality. I had a lot of pain in me from all the abuse and was carrying a lot of bad memories. I went into a very deep depression. All I could do was stare at the walls and cry. I couldn't deal with anything or anybody that reminded me of past problems. I was weighted down with financial responsibilities, failing health, family confusion, a troubled son and an ex-husband that continually harassed me.

Two days there and I didn't know my name or who I was. When I did come to my senses, I remembered that night in the hospital. It was 8 o'clock at night and there was another patient in my room with me and I asked her, "Where am I?" And she said, "Well, honey, I'm just as crazy as you are. I don't know." She hollered for the nurse to come and two nurses showed up. I asked them where I was. They informed me I was in Lakeside Hospital. They told me I had a nervous breakdown. I could remember Sheila, my friend, admitting me in there, but that is all I remembered. It was like a light came on inside of my head because then I realized where I was. That night the surroundings frightened me because I was in a room with bars like a jail. The nurses called the doctor.

He came in, sat beside my bed, and we talked for a long while. The doctor wanted to know about my life history. I told him what happened from childhood to the present; about all the pain and hurt I had experienced; about how I had kept it inside for so long. Then I begin to tell him about Rozen's death and about how he had just died the week before. The doctor said that Rozen's death is what had caused all these emotions to surface but it would also help bring closure to the past. He said, "For years you have had so much pain suppressed down in you and it has got to come out before you can ever get any better." He said, "Talking about it and counseling you is the beginning. I see dramatic trauma has happened in your life. You have tried to cover it up and it is eating you alive. Whenever you realize you can put your trust in someone that isn't going to hurt you then you can begin to heal. We are going to help you get well."

I then started going to meetings to learn about dealing with situations in life, depression, and why bad things happen to good people. During the meetings we would sit in a circle in the room and take turns talking about our problems. A lot of us had never talked about ourselves, but this was the beginning of our healing. After I went to a few meetings and listened to the stories of some of the other people, it didn't take me long to realize I didn't have a serious problem compared to most of the others. There were some real sick cookies in there. I couldn't believe some of the stuff I was hearing, so it didn't take me long to get myself together. I wanted out of there in a hurry because I realized I didn't belong in there; I wasn't crazy, I was just emotionally damaged. I got moved off of the crazy floor and put on a floor that had sane people on it that just needed a little counseling and encouragement. I got better after a few days and then I wanted to leave Lakeside. I didn't like being locked up because I had already had enough of that in the past. I admitted myself and I figured I could leave when I wanted to. By this time the doctors agreed I wasn't mentally sick, just emotionally drained. When I was admitted, I couldn't face another day of life. When I left, I felt like I could conquer my depression, and I could face the road before me. I realized I was strong enough to conquer the past and I started working on getting it together. It might have gotten me down for a few days but I came back up fighting harder than ever. I checked myself out of the hospital, and my friend Sheila came to pick me up. I wanted a new life and only I could make that happen. I lived with Sheila and Candy for a while and got stronger each day. I finally went back to work, cleaning houses and offices. We all three Sheila, Candy and myself had our own lives, but I wanted a home of my own. I was working and saving my money to buy a house.

So I came back to my hometown and bought a small 1400 square foot brick house with a large lot in the back. The house was all I needed to keep up with. I planted shrubbery across the front of the house and up and down the driveway. I built a picket fence across the front and kept my yard really neat. I was really busy working on projects for other people in the daytime and busy at night working on my house. I tried to stay busy to kill the empty void inside of me. I have always felt like work is a good policy to cure pain. I was still dealing with past mistakes but I knew one thing for sure I was not "nuts." I worked hard to stay strong and didn't think about the negative stuff. I buried myself in my work andprayed daily for God to help me.

My mental health was much better and the lupus was in remission. I only had to deal with the aches and stiffness of rheumatoid arthritis. I knew that God was gradually healing me. I had been single for about eight years now. Harry had moved on and was living with another woman. I had overcome a lot of the grief of my past mistakes and misfortunes. I wanted to improve myself, I wanted to look better, learn proper manners and improve my self-esteem. I wanted to have proper etiquette and to look like a real woman, prime, prim, and sophisticated. I didn't want to look like the sick girl any more that nobody wanted.

I enrolled in modeling school hoping to improve my self-image, not that I wanted to be a professional model, I just wanted to learn how to walk properly, look good, know table manners and how to act professional. It was a fun experience for an old plow girl like me because I needed all the help I could get. I graduated January 10, 1994 from Model World Modeling School.

I was holding my head up high and was feeling so much better about myself. And, I finally had a degree in something besides "cleaning." Before, I never thought I was pretty. Harry Sawyer had always beat it into my head that I was nothing but a cripple ugly SOB and nobody would ever want me. I prayed constantly to get that feeling off of me and now I am feeling the results. I worked hard at everything I did. I just needed to stay focused on positive thinking. I was feeling good now about my small decorating business and my new house that God provided for me.

Life was getting better. I couldn't afford a lot of pretty clothes or things I needed personally, things that women like to make themselves look and feel special. I had to pay my bills; I couldn't waste money. I was on my own and had nobody to help me. I went to yard sales on Saturdays and found pretty clothes and things I needed. I thought, "God is taking care of me." I always survived. Occasionally I would buy

Model World Graduate

This award of distinction is presented

To _KATHY TELSON_,

For Superior Achievement & Excellence of

Performance in _PROFESSIONAL MODELING_

This _10TH_ day of _JANUARY_, 19_94_

Signed _Darla Hall Caldwell_
Darla Hall Caldwell, Owner

MODEL WORLD Modeling School & Agency, 155 Carriage House Dr., Jackson, TN 38305 (901) 661-9551

Model Diploma

Kathy Telson
Hair: Auburn; Eyes: Hazel; Height: 5'9"
Measurements: 38-28-36; Dress: 8; Shoe: 8

myself an outfit at the dollar store when money was not so tight. I wanted good perfume, but I could only afford the dollar stuff. I was proud of anything, even if it was cheap or second hand. I was happy just for the small things in life; big price tags were not my style. I was so thankful I didn't have to put up with anymore abuse from anyone and to be in my right frame of mine. I realized I am somebody and that I am not as ugly as Harry had always tried to make me think I was. I had an inner beauty from God above and that was enough for me.

I knew the answer to healing my heart was that I had to forgive everyone who had hurt me. I had to get the bitterness, hate, anger and resentment out of me. This had eaten me like a cancer for years and I was ready to let go of it all. This garbage had made me literally sick. I worked at forgiving those who had wronged me one day at a time. I had to convince myself mentally to forgive Harry Sawyer, my mama, Lee Roy Telson, even my daddy, Mr. Floyd Edwards and last but not least myself. Hearing that Mr. Floyd Edwards was my daddy had caused me years of heartache; it would had been better if I had never known the truth or heard his name. Believing he was my real daddy never was a benefit to me except for causing me hurt and trouble. Because I knew this, I couldn't feel totally connected to my brothers and sisters or my mama. I paid a high price for years for finding this out. I couldn't understand why I never felt real love from them. I blame myself because whether it was my fault or not, I allowed it to create friction between us all. I am deeply sorry; it has been enough heartache to go around for all of us.

Time passed and I knew God was really working in my life, I just had to be patient. I trusted in God daily for guidance. It had been ten years since Harry and I had been divorced. I had totally forgiven Harry and had gotten rid of the gnawing cancer within my heart that was about to eat me alive. The hate and bitterness was gone for the suffering he caused me. It was not easy; it was a gradual process with God's help.

My son Jeff was still having a hard time with the past. He was a grown man; had a wonderful wife and three children. He worked hard and tried to provide for his family. He lived in a little mobile house trailer. Inwardly he was still hurting mentally, physically, and spiritually. I knew Jeff fought depression every day of his life. I felt so responsible for his wounded heart. I always tried to reassure him that in time all of his trouble would pass. I loved him with all my heart and soul. Jeff was the only man that I wanted in my life. I wanted to spend the rest of my life helping him get some closure for the things that had happened in his childhood. God had healed me and I tried daily to convince Jeff that God can help him also. I felt so guilty for putting that child through hell on earth from birth until sixteen. I prayed every day that God would restore his hurting heart. I believe I helped cause this pain by being a coward and not leaving Harry at an early stage of the abuse. All I could do was to keep trusting God to help my son and stand by him. Jeff was trying to get rid of the demons that were tormenting him, but he was struggling.

One day on a beautiful Sunday morning, Jeff came to church and sat on the back row. He hadn't been to church in years. I was so surprised to see him. My heart just rejoiced because I knew it was God's grace that got him there. It was a proud feeling to see him there. I got up and went back to where he was sitting, put my arms around him and told him that I loved him. He smiled back and said that he loved me too. Jeff started coming back to church regularly. Jeff had been cold and distant for a long time, but knew God was speaking to his heart, and I was praying for his damaged soul.

A month had passed and one Sunday night the preacher spoke on joy, love, and peace in your soul. I knew Jeff wanted to get free from the anger and hurt that tormented him every day of his life. Jeff was a good kid, but had a lot of pain going on within him and God was trying to get his attention. I could tell he was under strong conviction. Jeff stood and held on to the back of the pew while the pastor was giving the invitation to be saved. The pastor said that God was the answer to all heartaches and troubles. He said to just let Jesus in and heal your broken heart. Jeff knew God's spirit was drawing him to lay his burdens down. God was wanting to set him free. Jeff stood tall just crying silently. Finally he let go and walked to the altar of the church and bent down to pray. I went up and knelt beside him. He put his arm around me and said, "Mom, I am so tired of hurting." We prayed together and melted in the spirit of the Lord. We both knew that God was our only source. That night, he became a new man in the eyes of the Lord. God had ministered to his hurting heart. We got up from the altar and just hugged each other tight. I knew he was letting go of the past. He was God's child now.

A few months passed, Jeff was still doing well and pulling his family together. His wife Angie was so proud to see him smiling and loving her like he had never done before and involving himself with his three sons. Angie was always so kind and loving toward him. She had stood by him during all of their tough times. Angie was an angel from heaven sent to my son. I am very grateful for a good daughter-in-law.

Soon Jeff felt like he needed to make peace with his father. He went to see him and told him that he was living for Jesus. He told his dad that he forgave him for all the heartache he had caused. They began a good relationship after ten years of not communicating. Jeff invited his father to church and wanted to share the good news that Jesus is the answer. Harry started going to church with Jeff. After going to a few services, Harry accepted Jesus Christ. He asked God to forgive him for being a wicked man. Harry seemed to make a great change in his life and made peace with God.

Harry and Jeff came to see me one day. We all made peace with each other after having so much hate between us all. This hate and bitterness had already caused enough hurt for the three of us and I was glad to put it to rest. It was a good day; I was proud for Jeff and Harry. I waited for this day many years, and it finally came. Jeff wanted us to go to church together as a family. I didn't feel good about sitting with Harry on the same pew. I went anyway to please my son. Jeff had come through so much and I didn't want to cause him to stumble backwards. I did all I could to keep him happy and encourage him to stay in church. He needed to associate with strong Christian people.

18
A Mother's Love

Jeff came and talked to me alone. He said, "Mom, I know dad has made a big change in his life. He loves you so much. He is very sorry for the way he treated you in the past. He wants to make it up to you. Please give daddy another chance. I want us to be a real family. He wants to marry you again." I didn't feel anything for his father. I forgave him and just wanted peace. Jeff cried and begged me to give his dad another chance. He told me to at least pray about it. I hugged Jeff and as he was going out the door he said with tears in his eyes, "Please think about us being a family." I shut the door behind him and wept like a baby. I didn't want his dad in any way, form or fashion. I did not trust Harry at all. He might have made a change, but I still didn't have any feelings for him. I made peace with him because it was the right thing to do. I wished him well, but I just didn't want him back.

A few weeks passed and pressure was put on me big time. My brother, Dewayne, was a preacher at this time and he came and talked to me. He said, "Sister, Harry has been crying on my shoulder for a long time wanting me to help him get you to come back. I believe that Harry has made a big change in his life and, sister, he still loves you. I want you to think about it; you are in bad health, you need someone to take care of you, you are financially broke and you need to think about Jeff and the grandchildren. You have been single for a long time and who is going to want you sick and in this condition." He may have meant well, but it is really sad that he thought that low of me. I was paying my own bills and my health was getting much better. I thought I was in better shape than I had been in years. My son really wanted me to remarry his dad, and

Harry was trying hard as well. We started going out to eat as a family and going to church together. Lots of people were saying, "The past is the past, if God could forgive Harry, why couldn't I?" It did make me think.

Harry still had my clothes hanging up in his closet; the furniture in the house was just like I had left it ten years ago. Another woman had lived with Harry for several years, but he made her put her clothes in Jeff's bedroom closet. He wouldn't let her bother anything in his house. She knew that the house was just like I had left it, and my clothes were still hanging in the closet just like I had left them. Harry told her she could live there with him, and that he would take care of her but she was not allowed to move anything and he was not going to marry her. He only wanted companionship, and he was going to have his freedom; those were the rules, you either take it or leave it. She lived with him for several years in this lifestyle.

One day about a year before I left, Harry took my wedding rings off of my finger when he was really mad. He carried those rings wrapped up in a piece of paper towel in his billfold which he kept in his back pocket for ten years believing someday I was coming back to him. Harry had convinced me that he really did love me. I went to his house one day when I knew he was working and walked through the house just to see how I would feel. I almost fainted, I could not believe that everything was just like I had left it ten years ago. It was a feeling that I can not describe, it made me really sad, but then I thought this man is never going to give up on me.

I finally gave in and made an arrangement with Harry. I told him I was doing it for our son. That I cared about him because he was the father of our son and I forgave him for the past, but I could not love him like a wife was supposed to love her husband. I told him I was damaged material and God had to heal me before I could be a real wife to him. I didn't want him in that way. Jeff had a wife and three children; we would marry and try to rebuild the family for their sake.

It was the most painful thing I had ever done in my life. I felt like a prostitute that sold her soul to the devil. My heart was ripped to pieces battling with this decision. I hate to admit it, but I knew it was wrong when I was doing it, but I did it anyway for my son. I knew in my heart it wasn't God's will, but I was hoping for a miracle. I hoped and prayed that I was wrong about Harry, that he really was a changed man. I did not want to pay another high price for a terrible mistake. I thought if Harry was really a changed man, then maybe I could forget the past; that I could once again love him and we all could be a real family. I wanted to do what I thought was right, so that is why I bit the bullet and married Harry back after ten years of divorce.

Deep down I was hoping Harry was real; I knew I had to marry him back and give him a second chance. I had to see for myself, if I didn't, I would always feel the guilt of letting Jeff down without the chance of reuniting the family.

Harry moved in my house with me, Jeff and his family moved in Harry's house. Things were good for about two months and we were trying hard to be a family. I forgot about my own feelings and worked toward pulling us closer together. I tried hard but I never had the peace that it was right. Harry went to church with us for about two months and then he gradually got to slipping back to his old behavior. I was trying to keep my son happy. I have often said that I would lay down my life for my child; I love him so much. Harry and I had been married for three months before he started acting really strange. I had never trusted him and I just had the feeling that he was going to go off on me one day.

A church revival had been going on in Pensacola, Florida every night for several years. Many of our church members had gone and came back telling about how powerful God was moving in the church services. Television news stations were broadcasting about people from all over the world going there. I could sense Harry was beginning to drift back to his old mean ways. I convinced him that we needed to get with some Christian people and let them pray for us. Our marriage was getting rocky and we needed some help. I finally persuaded him to go to Pensacola. I was embarrassed to tell our church pastor what was going on between us since we had only been married three months and I knew in my heart trouble was on it's way. I did not want to go through another divorce and I wanted our marriage to survive.

Harry really didn't want to go but he said, "I'll take you anyway and I can stay at the motel while you go to church." Harry and I loaded up the car and we headed off to Pensacola to the church revival. It was about a day's drive. After driving for about three hours in silence I tried to start a conversation with Harry. I said, "Honey, please let's try to pull together and be like a family is supposed to be. We have already been through enough together and our only hope is God's help." Well, after I said that Harry went in a rage and said, "I am not putting up with your mouth, you had better shut up!" I replied back to him teary eyed, "Please don't act like that."

Harry pulled the car over to the side of the interstate and stopped. He got out of his side of the car, came around, opened up my door and hollered out, "Get the hell out, you are going to walk." I begged him not to do this, but he pulled me by the arm and put me out. I didn't have my purse, jacket or anything. Harry drove off down the road for about a mile and then pulled over and stopped. I could barely see the car and I was walking as fast as I could down the shoulder of the road. I was crying hard; cars and trucks were going by blowing their horns. I couldn't believe he had put me out on the interstate in the middle of God knows where. I finally got up to where Harry had stopped and I got back in the car, except this time Harry made me get in the back seat. If I had had any money on me, I wouldn't have gotten back in the car with the crazy thing, but I didn't have a choice. Harry was laughing; thinking it was funny, because he put me out.

We drove on and after dark we stopped at a rest area and slept in the car the rest of the night. Harry had a fit on him and would not spend the money for a motel room. I told him that I had money in my purse and would pay for the motel room, that I couldn't be cramped up in the car because it made my arthritis act up. Harry paid me no mind.

About daybreak we left the rest area and drove until we got to Pensacola. Harry pulled up to a motel and just sat there. I went in, rented a motel room and came back and told him what room we were in. I asked him to open up the trunk so I could get my luggage out. I got my luggage and went into the room. Harry never did come in the room, I didn't know where he was or what was going on, I just knew I was in a motel room all day long crying out to God to touch this man one way or the other. I must have been crazy because I had married this mad man back. About ten minutes till seven that night Harry walked into the motel room all smiles and says, "Lets go to church, girl." I looked at him and thought to myself, "You are a very sick man." He then told me he had been riding all day around Pensacola sight seeing. We got to church and he sat in there like a dead man.

The next day he got up about lunchtime, got ready and left again by himself and showed up at night just in time to go to church. Wasn't that a fine honeymoon trip! The next day we headed back home. Harry was just talking and acting like everything was fine. He said, "Yep, sure was some good church services and I really have enjoyed my trip." I thought, "Yea, the pressure is off of you now about going to God's house. That is why you are singing a different tune now." Harry was fine the rest of the way home; he even stopped and bought me lunch. This is just another chapter in our lives that I will never forget.

It was a cold day in November and I was feeling so depressed because

I was again living with a man I didn't feel comfortable with at all. Harry was starting to get more angry and was having a temper problem. I was really getting scared. So that night, he went off big time. Harry threatened that if I ever left him again, he would kill me this time. An awful feeling came on me and I wanted to lay down and die. I thought, I can't go through this again. I now realize it was all an act about Harry being a changed man just to get me back.

Here I was, with another round in hell. I couldn't believe this was really happening all over again. I must have lost my mind to have ever remarried him. I felt so embarrassed, ashamed, degraded, and I wanted to crawl in a hole, throw the dirt on myself and just die. I didn't know how I was going to ever survive this round. I tried to let my mind get focused on something positive, but the only thing I saw was the devil's den again. Harry was his old self again, getting mean just over small things. I couldn't please him no matter what I did. He was crazily jealous of me. He stopped me from going to the mailbox. He didn't want me outside the house. I guess he was afraid someone might look at me. He took my keys away from me, so I couldn't go anywhere. He would cuss, stomp and scream, "I will kill you this time! You better get that in your thick head!"

One of my friends came by and ate a hot dog for lunch with me. Harry comes in that night and wants to know who had been there visiting because he knew I didn't eat two hot dogs. Harry said, "I'm not going to feed the whole county, I will fix that." He put a chain around the refrigerator with a pad lock on it so I couldn't bother any of his food. If I touched one of his Dr. Peppers he would cuss. I was not supposed to touch anything of his that he bought. I thought that if he killed me, it was my fault for coming back to him. Harry would have a demon fit one day, and the next day act like nothing ever happened. He still had a split personality. He would put groceries up in the cabinets and write on the boxes, "Do not touch." I know it sounds crazy, but I knew he meant it. After the refrigerator deal I didn't bother any of his stuff, because I was scared of a beating. He had me so nervous and shaken that I didn't mess with him. Harry again owned me and believe me I knew it too. Many times I thought death was close by. Harry would cut the phone lines so I couldn't call and talk to anyone. I was a prisoner of his again. He was so angry that I had left him the first time and constantly brought up about me divorcing him and said that I would never get away again. I could see the demons in his eyes like flashing fire.

    Two or three days passed and Harry settled down somewhat. He was out back hoeing his tomato plants in the garden. As I watched him I wondered to myself how in the world he could be nice one minute and mean as the devil the next. I wish I could have helped him get his head clear.

    It was a hot summer day and I happened to look out the back door and noticed the hogs had escaped from their pen. I went out and began trying to get the hogs back into the pen. Harry was hoeing in the garden; he put his hoe down and we tried to run them back in the hog pen. Harry became so angry that he started yelling and went into a rage. He picked up a large stick from the barn, and I thought he might be going to hit me with it since he usually blamed me for everything that went wrong. Instead, a hog came his way. Harry began to hit him hard and continued to do so until the hog was completely dead. The demons were wild in him at this time. I was so scared that day that I wet all over myself. I had a habit of wetting on myself when I was extremely nervous or scared. Harry went back to hoeing in the garden. He just let the hog lie there in the hot summer sun.

    Two days passed away and the remains of the hog were still in the field. The live hogs were eating the remains of the dead hog. There was a knock at the door. The health department had received a call about us having a bad odor around our place. Two gentlemen were at the door and they said they had received a call about the foul odor around our place. They said, "We have to investigate to see what is going on." I knew it was trouble. I prayed they would take him to jail. They found the dead hog and asked questions. He told the gentleman the hog got out of the pen and so he taught it a lesson. They were amazed. They wrote a report on him and the health department left. Harry said that he would kick their asses if they messed with him or walked back into the pasture.

The next day he received a warrant to go to the court on animal cruelty. He was mad at me. I tried to reason with him so he wouldn't go off any worse. We went to court the next day and he only got a $1,000 fine and a probation warning. I thought that this man could get away with anything. There was a piece that came out in the weekly paper about Harry Sawyer and Animal Cruelty. I was so embarrassed when I read it, but I kept my mouth shut. There wasn't anything I could do about it. It was just another day of my life fighting the demons that came against me. Shivering under the covers, all I could do was pray for God to deliver me again.

Late one night Harry was doing some repairs on the house. He had been enclosing the carport for an extra room. He was working on the fuse box and he had the face cover off. When he started putting the cover back on the box there were a couple screws missing. He was cussing and hollering wanting to know what I did with them. I ran back there and I said "There is no sense in you cussing me all the time." He grabbed me and started choking me; threw me up against the fuse box and said to me, "I will cut your head off with the chain saw, boil your bones on top of the stove and bury your bones in the back yard and nobody will ever know what happened to you." The chainsaw was lying there in the floor within easy reach. In my mind I could hear it running. He told me that he would kill me this time and I believed him. The demons were so alive in Harry that night. When I looked into his face it did not have the appearance of a man, but of a wolf from hell. He was choking me so hard that I was beginning to turn blue and feeling like I was going to faint. I could barely grunt a word, but I was crying out to God, "Help me! Help me!" He finally let go of me and went out of the house. I knew this was when I needed to leave. It was around eleven o'clock at night and I was scared to death. I thought Harry was really going to kill me this time.

I had on a tee shirt, my jogging pants and a pair of socks. I found the keys to my truck and ran out the door like a scalded chicken. I drove so fast away from the house that it was a miracle I didn't wreck. There were two dollars in the ashtray of my truck, but I remembered the money in the old fruit jar I had buried in the ground under the old oak tree at my brother's house. I had hid the money several weeks earlier, anticipating it may come in handy. I had an inner feeling that things were going to get worse instead of better in my marriage.

I stayed all night with a girlfriend and never went back home to Harry. I had paid a high price for trying to make other people happy. We were married and divorced within five months this second go around. I was so embarrassed and humiliated over the bad mistake that I had just made, but thank God that I got out alive and that it was over.

In my divorce I signed my house over to Harry, he agreed to finish paying for it and our son would have it some day. All I wanted was the seven-piece cherry bedroom set that I had worked for years to pay for. I was totally disabled when we divorced, but I did not ask or want anything else. My lawyer wanted to clean his plow and make him pay me alimony and fix me up financially for life, but I chose not to. I wanted to be fair and I did not want anything from him. He had already given me enough heartaches to last for a lifetime. (There was no price that could ever repay the damage that I will carry to my grave.)

19
Mama Grace

For about two weeks I went from house to house and stayed with friends from church. The women of my church were going to a women's conference in Memphis so I went with them and roomed with three other ladies. They all could tell that I was so troubled. I asked them to pray with me that I could find a home, because I had left my husband. They prayed with me and showered me with love. When we came back I needed a new place to stay and a lady that had gone to the conference with us had helped me get into a low-income subsidized housing project. I moved into a one-bedroom apartment, number 209, for $178 per month. There was a handicap sign in the front yard of my apartment. It was the only thing available and that worked out great because of my health problem from the arthritis. It was a clean, neat place, and it was my home. It had an alarm system and this made me feel safe. All I had to do was push a button and help would be on the way.

Harry and I had been divorced for several months now; I wanted to go to mama's and see how she was and spend some time with her. I just needed to talk to her. I hadn't been since Harry and I had been divorced. I walked in her house and went back to the kitchen where mama was. I fixed me a cup of coffee and started to sit down at the table where mama was sitting. She was so cold towards me that day and her words were as deadly as a bullet through my heart. Mama said, "Hurry up and get that cup of coffee drunk and get out from here. Harry Sawyer will be driving by and I don't want you up here. I am old and I don't want any trouble." I got up from the table and said, "Mama, I have been through enough, why do you have to be so mean to me?" She replied, "You made your bed hard, you lie in it, I don't feel a bit sorry for you. Get out from here." I left heart broken as usual after a meeting with Mama. It was very obvious she still had no love at all for me.

As I was leaving and going down the road I met Harry going up to mama's house. He had a truckload of produce he was taking her to feed her ducks and chickens. She knew he was coming and he was more welcome than I was, because I was a poor girl barely making ends meet and I didn't have anything to give mama. It hurt so bad to think that her ducks and chickens getting fed were more important than seeing me. I was still like that little girl crying out, "Mama, please love me!" The empty void inside of me from the rejection of my mother was worse than anything I had gone through with Harry. Every child has a craving need to feel connected to it's parents and I can't seem to get it after all these years. But I still love my mama regardless of the rejection.

Therefore I say unto you, what things soever ye desire when ye pray, believe that ye receive them, and ye shall have them.
(Mark 11:24)

I will always pray, believe and hope for a miracle, that mama and I can resolve whatever it is that keeps us from having a normal mother and daughter relationship. Only God can do it.

I can remember the days in the apartment when I'd cry out to God for an answer to my emptiness. I prayed daily, "Lord, send someone into my life that I can feel love to the deep depths of my soul." I yearned to feel the love, the closeness of a mate that would understand me and accept me for who I was. I just wanted to be loved. I wanted God to open up the doors for me to have a loving and godly home.

Mama Grace, my next door neighbor at the apartment complex came and visited me the second day I was there. She said, "I am an eighty-five year old grandma and I'm here for you if you need me." She sat down in a chair and started talking. She said she had been praying that morning and the Lord told her to come over and give me a big hug. She opened her arms wide and said, "Come here child I want to pray for you." I went and knelt in front of her. She put her loving arms around me and prayed. It was like heaven came down. She got deep in the Spirit and pulled my head in her lap. She prayed over me and cried out "Jesus, take this child's pain away, she has had enough." I can feel her now as I am writing this book. Mama Grace was a prayer warrior like I had never seen before. She felt my hurt and all my troubles.

From that day on, Mama Grace and I stuck together like glue. That precious saint prayed for a great healing of deliverance for my soul. I never told her anything, she just knew by the Spirit of God that I was deeply burdened and troubled. We prayed a lot of nights until two in the morning. I know God put me there for that period of time in my life so she could minister to me. She helped me get through some bad times. I loved her dearly and miss her a lot.

She told me a few days before she died that she would be my angel coming back from heaven to watch over me. She told me she loved me. When I'm down and out I can hear her say, "Smile, Jesus loves you." I am so grateful that God put me next door to her. Her love, warmth, caring and sharing touched a lot of lives as well as mine. God put her in my life when I needed comfort and someone to care for me. Isn't God good? She prayed for God to heal me emotionally and physically and to rain His blessings upon me.

Harry came to my apartment one day while Mama Grace and I were sitting on the front porch visiting with each other. I was a little nervous when he walked up but I noticed he had really been crying. He said, "Kathy, I need to talk to you and I want to give your wedding rings back, I think after you married me twice you deserve them." I told Harry,

"You have taken those rings away from me after two marriages and two divorces from you, I don't want them or need them either." Mama Grace says, "Well, let's go inside and sit and talk." Mama Grace knew the history of him and me and when she saw him, she knew exactly who he was.

Harry broke down and told me he was so sorry for all the trouble he had put us through. He begged me to give him one more chance. He said he loved me and he would do anything I asked, including counseling, if I would just come back home. He was so pitiful. I started crying and I said, "Harry, I have given you chance after chance, I just can't do it, I am so sorry, you have got to accept it, it is completely over for good. You are the one that had caused this to happen again. I am not trying to make you feel any worse than you already feel. I tried hard and I really wanted it to work, but it was never meant to be. Please leave me alone."

Mama Grace said, "Harry, I'm not trying to butt into your business, but you need God in your life and He will help you. I know you are hurt, can I pray for you?" Harry said, "Yes mam." Mama Grace put her arms around him and prayed hard for God to touch his life. She showed Harry love and compassion and told him she would pray daily for him. She hated to see him in this bad shape. Harry got ready to leave; I walked up to him and hugged him with tears running down my face and said, "I am so sorry; it's over."

After a while I really began to feel God had healed me from the wounds of the past. Mama Grace had convinced me that if I didn't get rid of the anger and bitterness, and forgive all of those people that had hurt me I couldn't be healed. She knew it had been like a huge cancer inside of me for years and getting it all out was my way of letting go of the past mistakes and misfortunes. The trauma of the pain had controlled me long enough and made me literally sick in my body. I believe that is why I had been sick just about all my life and I was ready to let go of the

Mama Grace
"Great Prayer Warrior"

misery that had ruined my life.

I got down on my knees and prayed until I got all of the garbage out of me. I could honestly say, "Today I have completely forgiven everyone that had ever damaged my life." I had no hate, no hard feelings and no resentment toward anyone and most of all I prayed that those people would realize the harm they had caused me. "Revenge is the Lord's; you can't fight evil with evil." When I was so broken and shattered and when nothing else could help, only God's love had lifted me. God put a love in my heart and had healed me of all the mental, physical and sexual abuse of the past. "To God be the glory!" I knew my dark days were over and God had something special in store for my life.

I felt that all the chains of darkness had been lifted from me. I felt like a new woman that had undergone an over haul job on the operation table. I was seeing life different, I looked at myself in the mirror and I felt pretty. I felt good about who I was and where I was going. Thank God that old dirty feeling was in the river that had washed my soul pure as the driven snow. I held my head up now, I felt excitement as I walked and I felt joy in my spirit. I knew I had been delivered. I was now excited about being the new woman God had miraculously transformed me into!

20
Three Confirmations

Mama Grace and I started praying for a godly man to come into my life. I was now a whole person and I knew I could give love to a good mate like I never could before. I wanted a husband, but I wanted to know that he was sent from Heaven. I never wanted another man in my life unless I knew God had sent him to me. If I ever was to have someone in my life again, I asked God to give me confirmation that he was truly His plan for my life.

As I prayed, I told God I had three requests that I wanted Him to fulfill if I were to ever have another man in my life. I didn't want any more garbage in my life and I was going to wait on God to send me somebody. I didn't want to make any more mistakes because I had already messed up enough in my past. I didn't want to meet him at church, at a yard sale, at the grocery store or even on a Mission trip.

First, I wanted him to be a total stranger that God would put on my doorstep. Second, if this man was to be in my life, that he would be a praying man. He'd be close to the Lord and I would know that with our first encounter. Third and last, if I was supposed to be his wife, he would take me to the park, which was my favorite place to be alone with the Lord, to ask me to marry him. I didn't ask for wealth or social status, I just wanted someone to love me, care for me, respect me and live right. I had always had this saying, "I'd rather have love in a hen house, eating a piece of cheese on a nail keg, than the finest mansion on a hill." I got involved with church, visiting the elderly, doing things with my grandchildren and just trying to survive on my meager income, but I was happy.

In the latter part of December 1998, there was a man outside my apartment mowing the leaves. I went to the mailbox and when I came back this man turned his mower off and spoke to me. His name was Dennis; he had his own lawn and landscape service, and he took care of the grounds at the apartments. He seemed like he had a compassionate heart because I knew he often checked on the little old ladies that lived in the apartment complex. He asked, "What is a young girl like you doing living out here?" I told him that I was a poor girl and that I was on a low-income budget. I told him my name and that I had experienced some hard times in life. It seemed like his heart was touched once he understood my circumstances. We started talking about how cold it was and it was very cold, so I asked him if he would like a cup of hot chocolate. He said, "I reckon so, anything hot would taste good." So I went in and fixed us a cup of hot chocolate. I invited him in to sit for a spell and warm up.

Dennis started telling me about his family and that he had a brother in Dallas, Texas. He said his brother, Richard, was grieving because his wife had died from cancer two years ago. He described him as shy and quiet and said that he couldn't meet a woman even if he wanted to. He told me that Richard went to church every Sunday and taught the youth in Sunday School; that he was very active in the church and strong in the Lord. Dennis said that Richard had a son in college named Spike, so he was home alone. He also told me about his and Richard's hobby of collecting old toys. He said, "You're such a nice woman, I really would like for you to meet him."

Some time passed and Dennis called Richard and told him about me. Richard started calling me and we talked often for about four weeks. He told me about his life and I told him some about mine. I didn't want to blurt it all out; I was going to wait until I could see him in person to give him the complete details. We talked about the churches we attended and our families. I shared with Richard that I was a Christian and that I loved the Lord very much. I told him that I'd wait until I saw him one day, and then I'd tell him my life story. That's just the way I wanted it to be. Talking to him was so easy; it seemed like we had known each other forever. As we talked a strong bond began to develop between us. I can't explain the feeling that was erupting inside of me each time I talked with him, but it was different from anything I had ever experienced before. We would talk anywhere from four to five hours every night. I think his phone bill that month was about $500.00. He always said he was going to come see me, but we did not set a definite time to meet.

On February 1, 1999, at eight o'clock on a Monday night there was a knock on my door. When I went to the door, there was a man standing there. He said, "Hello, I'm Richard." I was in shock. I really had been praying that he would be everything I had imagined he would be. When I saw him I knew he was different from the average guy. I invited him in and asked him to have a seat. He stepped close to me, gave me a big warm hug and then he sat down. We had just met, yet I could feel the transfer of love between us, not just from the hug but within the room as we sat and talked. I thought to myself, "God, please don't let this be a hit and run."

I decided then to tell him about my past life. I felt like I had to tell him all about my childhood and troubled marriages before we started a relationship. I knew it might be strange, but I knew I had to be up front at the beginning. I didn't want any misunderstandings; I didn't want him to think I was misleading him. I told him that I didn't have much to offer him but myself. I informed him of my deep love for the Lord and my desire to live right, but as far as being financially secure or educated, I didn't have it. What you see is what you get.

He, then, broke into tears and said, "None of that matters to me. I want to tell you about my life. I had been married for almost thirty years and didn't have the best marriage either." He told me he had gone through difficult times that had put a strain on his marriage. He did not give me the details, because he did not want to be disrespectful. He had a job that required him to travel and be away from home a lot and that didn't help his marriage either. He told me that Marsha, his wife, was a good woman and he had a lot of good memories of her regardless of the tough times in their marriage. She was a good cook and a good mother.

She had been sick with cancer for two years. She had a large ovarian malignant tumor that was removed, after which the doctors gave her a 50/50 chance of recovery. She then started chemotherapy treatments. After eight or nine months the cancer had come back with revenge. The last six months of her life Richard had stayed home from work to take care of her and stay by her side. She had gone from one hundred and fifty pounds down to sixty pounds. He told me God had done a mighty healing between them while she was on her deathbed. She was his high school sweetheart, and he had loved her very much. As he was holding her hand, her last words before she died were barely a whisper, she said, "I love you." We both wept as he was telling me about their final months together. It was so heartbreaking, I thought, "I haven't been through anything like he has." He later told me that at her funeral, his associate pastor had told him that God would reward him for taking such good care of her during her illness.

Richard had his grieving period and was very lonesome. He told me he had been single for two years. He had special friends from church that had cared a lot about him and involved him in their activities. He had dated other women, but he felt God had someone very special for him. Richard said he was lonely and he wanted someone to love for a lifetime again. Like me, he wanted to know they were real and from God.

I thought to myself that here was a man with a very good education, financially secure, and had it all going for him. He could have had a career-minded woman, but God brought this man all the way from Texas to Tennessee and put him on my doorstep. This proved how the power of prayer really works, that God brought a man that had everything to an apartment with a handicap sign standing in the front yard, and God brought him right to my doorstep, at apartment "209". Isn't God awesome?

Richard also told me about his son, Spike, and how proud he was of him. Spike was attending Duke University and majoring in electrical engineering and computer science. When Richard finished with the story of his life, he said that nothing really matters about our past lives and that he felt like we were two lonely hearts meeting in the middle. As we were sitting there on the couch, Richard said, "I know it is strange, I am experiencing feelings that are blowing me away and I have just met you." He told me he felt like he had already fell in love with me over the phone.

It's about ten o'clock and Richard says he had better go. So I stood up in the middle of the living room, he walked up to me, put his arms around me and held me tight. He held me for a few minutes and then he started shaking. The Holy Spirit was all over him. This Baptist man started praying like something coming out of heaven. I was so touched and moved by the words of his prayer. When he finished praying, I prayed to God that night with such a joy coming out of my spirit that I knew right then that God had put us together. After we had finished praying he looked me right in the eyes and said, "Kathy, you are the angel that I've been praying for. I'll see you tomorrow." He left that night to go stay with his parents who lived in another town about fifteen miles away.

That entire night I praised God for sending him my way. I knew in my spirit that he was real and God had sent him. I had never experienced the kind of emotions that were within me and I knew it seemed extremely strange because it was the first time I had ever met him.

The next day he sent me a dozen of the most beautiful long stem red roses. I had never gotten roses in my life that were so precious to me. I was so touched and moved, I couldn't believe it. On the card it said, "I love you." That night we planned a dinner date and Richard was coming to pick me up at seven. I was so excited as I was preparing to get dressed for my date. I took a long hot bubble bath and tried to relax as I lay in the bathtub thinking of him. I felt like the events of the last twenty-two hours were a wonderful dream. All I could do was say, "Thank you, God" over and over. I was having myself a shouting time as I was getting ready.

I wanted to look my best. I put on my black dress slacks with a light green turtle neck top and a short black dress jacket that went to my waistline. I put on my black three inch dress heels; I wanted to look sharp. I fixed my hair so it would look soft and natural. Richard had previously told me on the phone that he didn't like to feel stiff hair. I put on very little makeup and spicy red lipstick because I just wanted to look good and be myself.

After I finished getting dressed, I went next door to Mama Grace's to let her see how I looked. She said, "Child, you will catch his eye tonight." I said, "Mama Grace, I don't have any good perfume, all I have is that dollar store stuff." She laughed a little bit and said, "We can take care of that." She went into her bedroom and brought back her good perfume; she sprayed some in my hair and dabbed some on my wrist. She said, "That ought to do it." She was so proud for me because this was a prayer answered, that she and I had prayed for. She hugged me as I was leaving to go back to my apartment next door. She said, "I will be praying for you tonight and y'all be good." She then said, "Take your little New Testament and put it in your purse. If Richard gets to feeling froggy, tell him he has to jump over Matthew, Mark, Luke and John." Mama Grace always had a comical sense of humor. I kissed her bye and told her. "I'll tell you all about it tomorrow." I was on cloud nine knowing I had a real date.

About seven o'clock my door bell rang, I opened the door and Richard said, "Well, hello there beautiful." I was so overjoyed to see him, he gave me a hug and I could tell that he was just as excited as I was. We walked to his truck; he opened the door for me and held my arm to help me up into the seat. I thought, "Wow, he is a real gentleman, this surely is different from where I had come from." We went to a nice restaurant for dinner in the next town. The restaurant was crowded and we had to wait a while to be seated, every eye there was on us. Richard did look sharp that night, he is six foot tall, with salt and pepper hair and he was dressed like a rich Texas oil man. "Honey, let me tell you, he was refined." We couldn't take our eyes off each other.

 We finally were seated at our booth, so he didn't get to push my chair up for me. The waiter came and asked if we would like an appetizer. Richard asked me what I would like to have, of course I didn't know what an appetizer was and said, "Just pick something out for us," I didn't want Richard to know I was that "green." I had never been anywhere where they served appetizers; I didn't know if it was a drink or a dessert. I just didn't know! After a few minutes our waiter brought our ice tea and an appetizer. The appetizer looked like a bunch of fish tails battered in meal, it was called coconut shrimp, I ate one and told Richard it was delicious. But it didn't matter to me what it tasted like, I was just glad to be with him. Richard had ordered each of us a big juicy steak, but we hardly ate anything that night, we were both just too excited about seeing each other.

 After dinner we went to the City Park to walk and talk. I was so amazed he wanted to go to the park because it is my favorite place, a place where I often go and spend time alone with the Lord. We held hands tightly as we walked very close together, sometimes walking with our arms around each other. The night was cold and crisp, it was about midnight by this time and too cold to be outside walking. We went back to the truck, sat and talked for a long while and then decided it was getting too late to be in the park. Richard drove slowly going home, "with me sitting as close to him as I could get." He said that I was the girl he had dreamed about so many times and now it was a reality, here we were!

We arrived back at my apartment; he opened his door and held my hand as I slid out on his side of the truck. He walked me to the door, kissed me goodnight and told me, "I love you, you're everything I have ever wanted, I've got to go, I'll see you in the morning." He left to go stay all night with his parents. I watched him get in his truck and as he drove off he waved. As I closed my door, I hollered, "Thank you Jesus." I had myself a Holy Roller shouting spell; I knew that God was working on my behalf.

Richard came back the next morning about eleven o'clock, we had only a short time left to spend together because he had to leave late that afternoon to go back to Texas. I was sad, but I said to the Lord there was no rush about anything. I just wanted to be in God's will, I knew time would tell a lot for us.

Richard was gone for two weeks, but he called every morning and every night. We really did miss each other. After two weeks, he was back in Tennessee. He said he couldn't stand being away from me any longer; I sure was beginning to feel special by now. He stayed for about three or four days this time and then left for Texas again. It was becoming very hard for him to leave me, we both knew we had seriously fallen in love with each other. But knew we needed more time before making any definite future commitments. Before Richard left he said, "Let's be in prayer about our future." He kissed me very passionately, said, "I love you," and was gone again.

Six weeks had passed since our initial meeting. Richard wanted me to come to Texas to meet his friends and visit his church. He wanted me to fly, but I was nervous about flying, so I decided to ride a Greyhound

Apartment "209"
"God puts a stranger on this doorstep"

bus. I didn't want to drive either because I knew I couldn't drive in a big city. My best friend, Mary Ellen, took me to the bus station and made sure I got on the bus safely. I was so excited I couldn't think straight on my own. I just put my head up against the bus window as we were traveling down the road and thinking how fortunate I was to have met Richard, I knew in my heart that he was a good man and I was madly in love with him. Life really felt good right now.

The bus ride didn't seem long at all getting to Texas. I would have driven a team of mules and a wagon to get there to see Richard if that were the only way. I just knew I had to get to Texas to see my "sweetie." I wasn't nervous at all riding a strange bus, just full of joy and excitement. There was a girl on the bus who was acting distraught; she was talking loud and was drinking from a milk of magnesia bottle. The bus driver pulled the bus off on the side of the road and stopped. He got out of his seat and went back to the back of the bus where she was sitting to see what her problem was. She was drinking whiskey concealed in the milk of magnesia bottle and had apparently been drinking for some time because of the way she was acting. I overheard the bus driver say he would have to put her off the bus at the next stop. I talked to the driver and asked him if he would let me talk to her and try to calm her down. He agreed and went back to his seat and we were on our way. The girl was really broken hearted because she had just been through a divorce. I sat and talked to her for the rest of the way to Dallas. I listened to the heartaches and troubles she had gone through. I thought about how many women there are in this world that have so much pain from broken homes. I was so thankful I was there to help her in a time of need.

As we were getting close to Dallas and I was looking out the window I saw roads on top of roads. There must have been five or six. I was just in awe, I thought I had been to the city before, but nothing like this. It was a sight to see. I was amazed at the multitude of highways. What a change from the country roads of Tennessee! I came from the country where there were mostly one or two lane roads and I had never seen anything like this before. It was all new territory for me. I said, "God really did something when He put these roads together." The bus driver said "Child, where did you come from"? I said "From the sticks," he chuckled and said, "I believe you did."

I arrived in Dallas Texas late Friday night; Richard met me at the bus station with open arms. I couldn't believe that a man like this who had everything really loved a poor girl like me. This seemed so unreal to me. I knew God put him in my life. God had already fulfilled two of my three requests. First, he put him on my doorstep and secondly, Richard prayed with me on our first encounter. I didn't know the kind of treat I was in for that weekend in Texas. I know it was all a part of God's plan. I was so touched when I saw him. I just melted. He got my bags for me. We got in his truck and left downtown Dallas. We got to his house and I was awed by the size of his house. We sat in the truck in the driveway and he put his arms around me and said, "I'm so glad you came to visit me." He also told me that he loved me. That was about the third or fourth time he told me. He said it that night with such power in it. I mentioned how beautiful the house was and asked him who his neighbors were, because I thought there was another house very close to his. He said that was not another house but was part of his house. I was in shock.

Everything was happening so fast. I felt like Heaven's doors were swinging wide open for me to come on in. I knew I was finally being loved like a normal human being. We walked around to the front door. The Spirit of the Lord came upon me and said, "Welcome to your new home." I started shaking and crying. Richard put his arms around me as I was crying and told me that he loved me so much. He then said, "Welcome to your new home." It blew me away because the Lord had just spoken that to me. It was about all I could take, I was about to have

Plow Girl Goes to Dallas, Texas

a shouting spell.

He opened the door and I saw the marble floors in the foyer. I was amazed and cried even more. We stood in the foyer for about an hour or two because I couldn't stop crying. The Spirit of the Lord had just come upon me. I kept thanking Jesus over and over again. After my crying spell, we sat on the couch in the living room. I felt such a safe haven here, like I had never felt before. We talked a little bit. By then, it was four in the morning. He got my bags from his vehicle and put my things in the guest bedroom that was enormous. He told me that he was right down the hall if I needed him, and we'd have breakfast in the morning.

He woke me up the next day by kissing me. He said, "Good morning sweetheart. You look so beautiful in the morning!" I thought that I looked like a dog! I was so overwhelmed with my love for him. I got up and took a shower and got ready for the day. When I went into the kitchen he had my coffee and toast ready. We had a joyful day on the town.

That Saturday night he wanted me to meet some of his friends. He told me that they lived in a big house, but they were regular people just like us. I knew that Norma and Chris Fitts were country folks like me when Richard described them. I was not going to try to be a different person just because they lived in a nice house. I just wanted to be my natural self.

Saturday night we ate with his friends at their house. It was time to sit down at the table. We had spaghetti, salad, bread, and dessert that night. They had a salad bowl sitting on the plate so when the spaghetti was passed to me, I put it in the salad bowl. I was just nervous and not thinking. When they passed the salad around, I just said I didn't want any. I was so embarrassed. I started watching how they were eating their food. They were cutting the spaghetti like it was steak and they'd twist it around on a spoon. The only way I knew how to eat spaghetti was to slurp it up from the fork. I knew I had to learn better manners. I felt as if every eye was on me and I am sure they were. I asked if I could be excused to go to the bathroom because I was so nervous. Before I went, I accidentally knocked a glass of water over on the table and it went in Richard's lap.

That's when I knew I needed to be excused. I got up and went to the bathroom and prayed, "Lord, I am so nervous. You've got to help me. I don't know them and they don't know me and I know they're checking me out. Please make this a good night to remember." I'm sure they remembered that night because it was so unique. After my prayer I went back to the table. Everyone was finished so we just had refreshments and cake.

After that, we went into the living room and talked for a spell. I knew I had made a mess out of the night by knocking the water over and putting my spaghetti in the salad bowl. Richard thought it was about time for us to go and I was glad. Everyone hugged me and told me they were glad to meet me. I asked them then if they would like to join hands and pray. They all looked at each other in shock. That's all I knew to do was pray. We joined hands and I prayed like I had never prayed before. I guess I thought I could preach that night because I was so happy, I just really prayed.

After that we left. When we got into the truck Richard said, "I'm going to take you somewhere very special." I thought we would just go riding around in Dallas because it was just so big. He took me to a very big, beautiful park. It had a big pond in the middle.

The night was cold, damp and windy but we were so in love with each other that even if it was ten below zero it wouldn't have made a difference. My heart started beating really fast whenever we started walking around the park. I thought to myself, "Is this going to be my third confirmation?"

We walked half way around the park and when we came to a bench, Richard told me to sit down on it. He hugged me really tight and then got down on his knee and said teary eyed, "Kathy, I know that this is quick and I don't understand a lot that's going on except I know that I'm madly in love with you. I truly believe that God has smiled upon us and put us together. Will you be my wife?" He, then, pulled out a big diamond marquise ring and I just broke into tears. I just kept saying yes, yes, yes! We hugged and rolled on the ground and almost into the water. That was such an experience in my life. Going to the park was my special place because it's where I spend time with the Lord and it's where I'm writing this book also. So God gave me my third confirmation. I knew that I was going to be his wife.

After that night I felt like I was floating. It was as if I was dreaming. God really gave me what my heart desired. I couldn't believe that a poor girl like me would have a man that really loved her and a good life. After that night an inner healing started taking place. Before, I could never feel the love or what I needed, but I felt it this time. I knew that it was real. I knew that he was heaven sent. And every day of my life I thank God for him. I know God can do anything.

That Sunday morning he took me to his church and before we went in he said. "Honey this church is a little different than what you are used to, they don't shout here, and you may feel out of place." I knew what he was trying to tell me because us Pentecostals get down in the Spirit and the Baptists are more formal, at least those Baptist were. I always believed if you can holler and hoop at a ballgame then you ought to be able to holler and hoop for Jesus anywhere. There were about two thousand people at church that day and I could feel every eye on me. I was holding my head up high with a big smile. I felt so proud to be hanging on Richard's arm because I knew there were women there that had been after him and here I was with him. All I could say under my breath was

"Thank you Jesus." I felt so special that day; I felt like I could fly.

I got back on the bus that Monday morning and headed back home. I was so excited with happiness as I rode the bus going back to Tennessee. I just started thanking Jesus for my life that I knew was about to take place. The Greyhound bus stopped in a little town called Hope, Arkansas and picked up two men that looked rough. They got on the bus and I looked at them and sensed trouble, I mean with a capital "T". The bus was loaded except for the seat next to me and the seat behind me. Well one of the guys sat down behind me with a lady that had a baby in her arms and the other guy looked at me and said, "move over" with a rough tone in his voice. So I moved over and he sat down next to me. He had long dark dirty hair, looked like he had not had a bath in days and was wearing boots. He put a big bag in his lap as the bus started moving on down the road. All of a sudden he looked at me eye to eye and said, "You are with me." I thought what kind of stuff is he on today; he has got to be out of his mind. I was just in shock. I was crowded in next to the window of the bus and no way to move, so here we go lick-a-dee split down the road.

I looked down at his feet and there was a gun sticking out of his boot, I didn't even think. I jumped up, put both hands up in the air and started shouting "Jesus, Jesus." I thought it was time to call on somebody I knew that could help us. While all of this was going on the bus driver pulled the bus over on the side of the road and stopped. When I finally calmed down I realized two guys and a dog had gotten on the bus. I did not know what was happening until they had walked past me going towards the back of the bus and I saw on the back of their jackets the word "bounty," that was all I could make out. One of the guys turned around and told the man sitting with me to stand up. He stood up, they hand cuffed him and they also hand cuffed the man behind me. They opened up his bag and it was full of white stuff that looked like sugar. The bad guy looked at me and said, "You are a freak." I said, "Well, you are the one getting hand cuffed, not me." I reckon I took care of him with God's help. He apparently had never heard a shouting woman before. After that they got off the bus and we were on our way. Everybody on the bus was just in awe over what had happened. I finally got back home to Tennessee and that was my last bus ride. What an experience to remember!

21
Midnight- Knock On The Door

I waited to let Richard tell his family about us. I was quiet and only told a few girlfriends of mine about our relationship. I knew that we were supposed to be married someday but it would be hard for everyone to understand, especially his family.

His family was on a higher social level than mine, which was true. They thought they were at least. I knew they were never going to accept me. It was really his mother, Mrs. Zora that didn't care for me. When Richard was away in Texas, he wanted me to go down to her house and meet her. I went and knocked on the door; I knew she was expecting me because Richard had told her about our relationship. He told Mrs. Zora that he was in love with me, but we didn't know when we were going to marry. She let me in and gave me the third degree. She was worse than the FBI when it came to checking out my background. She wanted to know why my previous marriages had failed. Mrs. Zora asked me if I was such a strong Christian, then why didn't I pray a little harder for my ex-husbands to change so I could stay away from her son. She was very mean, bitter and angry. She didn't think that I was fit or sophisticated enough to be in their high society family. She didn't want us to be together, and she didn't understand how God had really put us together. She was very rude, angry and hard on me that day. After I took her hateful treatment for about thirty minutes, I decided it was past time to leave. I told her that I'd pray for her and wished she could understand how Richard and I felt about each other. As I left she kept yelling, hollering, and pointing her finger at me to come back and listen to what she had to say. She kept saying,"leave my son alone, you hear me." I went on my way. I was very hurt that day, but I was determined that

Richard and I were supposed to be together. After that I went back to my apartment and told him on the phone about my meeting with his mother. We knew all we could do was pray for Mrs. Zora and hope that she would eventually accept our love for each other.

The next week I was leaving to go on a mission trip to Victoria, Mexico. I had to put aside for a while what was going on with Richard and his mother. I needed to prepare for my trip. I went to Mexico with a group of people from my church and several other churches; there were about a hundred that went on the trip. It took thirty-six hours on the church bus to get there. We went to build a church and minister to the poor and needy. We took clothes and food to help the poor families. There were homes there that were made of nothing more than cardboard boxes. The children were so raggedy. It was so sad. It felt so good to go out and help people so needy.

One night after we had gone back to our rooms at the little hotel, there was a knock on my door. It was the hotel clerk and he handed me a piece of paper. It was a fax from Richard saying he loved me and he was praying for our group while we were in Mexico. I was so surprised because I did not know he knew how to get in contact with me. He knew one of the men on our trip from Missouri that I did not even know. Richard had called his friend's office to see if there was a way to make contact with members of the mission group and finally after several calls to different people he found out the fax and telephone number of the hotel where we were staying. The next night Richard called me at my room and told me that he loved me; I just hollered because I was so proud to hear from him. Our mission team stayed in Mexico a week before we came back home. The bus came back to Memphis, Tennessee and we were all so tired from the thirty six-hour ride back home.

Richard came all the way from Texas to meet me at the church parking lot In Memphis when I got off the mission trip. Twelve weeks had passed since we started dating each other. It seemed like we had known each other forever. We spent the next two days together talking and planning. At night, he would stay with his parents. He kept trying to convince Mrs. Zora that we loved each other and wanted to get married, but she was so against it. Richard stayed in Tennessee about three days before he went back to Texas. He was very sad when he left, because he knew he loved me and having his mother's blessing would make our lives much more pleasant.

It was holy terror on his mother's part, because Mrs. Zora thought I would be a disgrace to their family. Mrs. Zora had called several of the people that I went to church with to check me out including some of the staff. She got in touch with the ex-husband and asked questions; she then cornered my son Jeff at the local grocery store and tried to pry all the information she could out of him. She must have checked at the county courthouse to see when and how I had married and divorced. She would have been a pretty good investigator for the FBI. She was bound and determined to stop this marriage. Richard and I had different backgrounds and she was troubled about that. When he got home, he called and told me that it didn't make any difference what his family thought. I knew in my heart that we would be married one day, but I didn't want to come between Richard and his family. I told him that we should call things off for a while so things could get cleared up. I told Richard that I'd send him the ring back. Richard broke down and started crying on the phone, he told me that he loved me and not to do this to us. I just didn't want to be in the middle of him and his family. I loved Richard very much, but I was very hurt. About two or three days passed and I wouldn't answer the phone when he called, because I was in a lot of pain. I had already had enough heartache and I sure didn't need any more from Richard's mean old mother. I couldn't help it. I needed some time to think about all of it.

On Thursday April 15th at about midnight, there was a knock at my door. I went to get the door and Richard was there unexpectedly. I asked him what he was doing; he hugged me and cried. He told me he loved me more than anything, and nothing was going to get in the way of our love for each other. Richard said that he came to get me and that it didn't matter what anyone else thought. He told me that we were going to go to Little Rock, Arkansas the next day to get married. He said he didn't care about what his family would say, he loved me and that we'd spend the rest of our lives together happy. We could work through all of this together through the power of prayer. I agreed with Richard and I didn't want to let him go.

Richard and I went next door and got Mama Grace up to council with us. She prayed with us for a long time and said, "There is no doubt that God has put you two together to do a work for him, don't let anybody stand in the way." We stayed there until about five in the morning. We went back next door to my apartment, took showers and got dressed to head to Little Rock, Arkansas.

I didn't have anything fancy to wear for the wedding, except my best Sunday dress that I had gotten at a yard sale for ten dollars. We left at about six thirty that Friday morning, April 16, 1999. When we got close to Little Rock, we stopped at a little rest stop and changed clothes; he into his suit and I into my Sunday dress. I was so happy; I had never known this feeling before. We went to the courthouse there and got our marriage license. Richard asked if there was a Justice of the Peace near by so we could get married at someone's house that could say a word of prayer over us. We really didn't want to get married in a courthouse. We got our marriage license, got the number of a lady that was a retired justice of the peace, called her to make sure she was home and looked her up.

There had been a tornado in her area recently that blew every house away on that block except for hers. We knocked on her door and told her who we were. She invited us in and asked us what kind of ceremony we wanted. We could tell that she was a strong Christian, a praying woman. We told her that we wanted a word of prayer for us. She had us to join hands in front of her fireplace and she proceeded with the ceremony. Of course she said a word of prayer afterwards.

I was one of the happiest girls in the whole wide world. I knew someone truly loved me and has accepted me for who I am. I was finally going to have a real home. I could feel the peace and joy within me and the love coming from Richard. All my heartaches and hurts had vanished away. I felt like Cinderella that day.

Richard had already made reservations at the Double Tree Hotel in Little Rock. We left the lady's house that had married us and on the way to the hotel, Richard stopped a young man that was walking down the street and asked him where the nearest grocery store was. Richard told him that we had just gotten married and that he had to get some cheese, crackers and strawberries to take to the hotel. I was so embarrassed. The young man giggled; told us where the grocery store was and said, "Y'all have a good time." We went and got our groceries and then to the hotel.

We hibernated for three days in the honeymoon suite in Little Rock and that's all I can say about that. Some things are just private. After our honeymoon we loaded up and went back to my apartment in Tennessee. We stopped and got a U-haul trailer, hooked it up to the truck, went to my apartment, loaded everything I owned and headed back to Texas. We didn't waste any time hanging around in Tennessee because there wasn't anything but trouble there for us.

On the way to Texas we passed through Memphis where Richard called his brother using his cell phone. He said to Dennis, "I just called to tell you that I'm married. I'll talk to you later." That's all that he said. He couldn't share the wonderful day we had because they were so against it. Richard's family thought I was just poor white trash, and I wasn't good enough for him because of where I came from.

We were off to Texas. As I crossed the state line between Tennessee and Arkansas, I said to the Lord, "Thank you for my new life. I don't want to look back anymore. I just thank you for this day." On the way to Texas we stopped and stayed in a honeymoon suite again. We just enjoyed each other. The next day we kept driving toward Texas. We finally got home to Dallas, Texas. We were like two little lovebirds, laughing and giggling. We were having such a good time; it was like a fairy tale, but thank God, it was real.

A month passed and we decided to go back to Tennessee to visit my son and Richard's family. It was very hard to meet Mrs. Zora again for the first time as Richard's wife. I was married to him now and even though his mother didn't approve of it, she had to accept the fact that we were married now, whether she liked it or not. The first visit was rough, but we got though it. She sure didn't make me feel welcome in the family. Every day we put our hands on Mrs. Zora's picture; prayed and asked God to soften her heart. We wanted her to see how happy we were together. We wanted her to know that we loved each other very much and wanted to be a family. I knew that it was going to be a hard long road ahead of us, but we were willing to plow through it because we were praying for a miracle. Richard knew I had never had a close family and he wanted to share his family with me, but it didn't quite turn out that way. Richard and I were very happy with each other and knew that God had put us together. We also knew that strong praying would change his family.

It has been over three years since we were married and it has been a hard battle, being in this family, because of Mrs. Zora's resentment toward me. She has begun to soften her heart a little towards me. She saw that I am real and that I have a compassionate heart to help others. As of today Mrs. Zora is 79 years old and is a little kinder toward me. She realizes that her son is very happy with me. I believe she finally sees the true person that I am. She has asked me to forgive her for being a mean old woman. Mrs. Zora knows Richard and I love each other and is trying to accept our marriage. I forgive her for the anguish she put me through. Within time things will work out between all of us. Prayer does change lives and situations!

22
Shattered Glass

God has given me strength to put the pain, suffering and heartaches of many abusive years behind me. He has healed my mind, my body, my heart and my spirit. He has taught me most of all to forgive. Not being able to forgive is like a cancer that will eat and destroy you to the very depths of your heart and soul. If you don't forgive you can't truly be delivered from the pain of your past or be able to completely enjoy the blessings God has for you. Jesus Christ saved me at an early age. He has put a burning desire to live for Him in the root of my soul and I can feel his spirit within me daily. I can feel the call of God on my life to speak out and touch other abused and battered women.

I have also written this book because I felt I had to get it all out of my mind, heart and soul. It has been a time of healing as I wrote each word, each thought, each sentence. As I wrote, each teardrop that literally flowed from within me was washing the windows of my soul. I had a lot of hurt in me and I suffered extreme pain, both mentally and physically from the years of abuse, both as a child and as a young married adult. This book is the final chapter of my healing process. It was only through the power of prayer that I was able to put into words what my mind had locked away and unwilling to freely reveal.

Many abused women are like me; they keep believing, hoping and praying that their mates will change someday. We try to help them, but we just keep taking the abuse and continue to hurt ourselves. No one can tell an abused woman what to do in the time of her crisis, because we are hopelessly bound to our fate. Sometimes we even feel that we are the blame. We have mixed emotions, running scared, no place to go, no money, too embarrassed to get others involved and no family to turn to in the time of our troubles. I was a battered woman mentally and physically. I was in the state of mind that I did not want to live, and I did not want to die. I had to get to the point in my life that I was desperate for a change one way or the other. Only I could do anything about it and only I could take the first step with God's help.

I want to dedicate this book to all of the brokenhearted women and men in the world to say there is hope in the power of prayer. You have to come to the reality within yourself and say it is mind over matter, have faith you will succeed and do something about it before it is too late. When you come to the point in your life and ask, "Why doesn't God do something," just remember to keep your faith, stay focused and remember the promise God gave us, "There is eternal life in Jesus Christ for those who trust and believe in Him."

Everything I have been through has made me a stronger person in life. For what the devil meant for harm God will use for His glory to touch other hurting women. Don't ever give up, put your hand to the plow, hold your head up and walk by faith. You can make it and God won't let you down. I only asked God for love in a hen house, eating a piece of cheese on a nail keg, but I am blessed with much more.

Today I am like a shattered glass that was broken into many pieces and then miraculously put back together again, one piece at a time. This glass will never again be like it once was. It has a sparkle that shines like a new polished diamond, a walk that can climb any mountain, a determination that can overcome any of life's stormy seas and a peace that only comes from walking faithfully with the Lord.

May God richly strengthen every person who reads my life story.

Believe in a miracle!

KATHY WINGO

EPILOGUE

All of the Telson children were trained to work hard, keep our mouths shut, stay out of trouble and fend for ourselves. We have always been highly respected in our community for our hard work.

Several of my brothers have become very successful in the business world. Donnie, one of my younger brothers, now owns the old Whiterose School House where we worked in the cafeteria to pay for our school lunches. We often go there and proudly play basketball in the gym. My brother can now wear his cowboy boots on the gym floor without someone yelling, "Hey Telson, get off the gym floor with those cowboy boots on!"

Jeff and Angie have been married twelve years. Angie is now a registered nurse and Jeff works for a local trucking company.

My mother is eighty years old and is still very active on the farm. I have forgiven her for the past misfortunes between her and me. My relationship with her is slowly and gradually trying to heal. I still love my "Mama" very deeply.

Author's Contact Information

A Shattered Glass
P.O. Box 10875, Jackson, TN 38308
ashatteredglass@bellsouth.net